D1129070

The Treasure of Guadalupe

Celebrating Faith
Explorations in Latino Spirituality and Theology
Series Editor: Virgilio Elizondo

This series will present seminal, insightful and inspirational works drawing on the experiences of Christians in the Latino traditions. Books in this series will explore topics such as the roots of a Mexican-American understanding of God's presence in the life of the people, the perduring influence of the Guadalupe event, the spirituality of immigrants, and the role of popular religion in teaching and living the faith.

The Way of the Cross: The Passion of Christ in the Americas
    edited by Virgil P. Elizondo
Faith Formation and Popular Religion: Lessons from Tejano Experience
    by Anita De Luna
Border of Death, Valley of Life: An Immigrant Journey of Heart and Spirit
    by Daniel G. Groody
Mexican Spirituality: Its Sources and Mission in the Earliest Guadalupan Sermons
    by Francisco Raymond Schulte
The Virgin of Guadalupe: Theological Reflections of an Anglo-Lutheran Liturgist
    by Maxwell E. Johnson
The Treasure of Guadalupe
    edited by Virgilio Elizondo, Allan Figueroa Deck and Timothy Matovina

The Treasure of Guadalupe

Edited by Virgilio Elizondo,
Allan Figueroa Deck, and Timothy Matovina

ROWMAN & LITTLEFIELD PUBLISHERS, INC.
Lanham • Boulder • New York • Toronto • Oxford

ROWMAN & LITTLEFIELD PUBLISHERS, INC.

Published in the United States of America
by Rowman & Littlefield Publishers, Inc.
A wholly owned subsidiary of The Rowman & Littlefield Publishing Group, Inc.
4501 Forbes Boulevard, Suite 200, Lanham, Maryland 20706
www.rowmanlittlefield.com

PO Box 317
Oxford
OX2 9RU, UK

Copyright © 2006 by Rowman & Littlefield Publishers, Inc.

All rights reserved. No part of this publication may be reproduced,
stored in a retrieval system, or transmitted in any form or by any
means, electronic, mechanical, photocopying, recording, or otherwise,
without the prior permission of the publisher.

British Library Cataloguing in Publication Information Available

Library of Congress Cataloging-in-Publication Data

The treasure of Guadalupe / edited by Virgilio Elizondo, Allan Figueroa Deck, and
Timothy Matovina.
     p.   cm.— (Celebrating faith)
   Includes bibliographical references (p.   ).
   ISBN-13: 978-0-7425-4856-5 (cloth : alk. paper)
   ISBN-10: 0-7425-4856-2 (cloth : alk. paper)
   ISBN-13: 978-0-7425-4857-2 (pbk. : alk. paper)
   ISBN-10: 0-7425-4857-0 (pbk. : alk. paper)
   1. Guadalupe, Our Lady of.   2. Mary, Blessed Virgin, Saint—Apparitions and
miracles—Mexico.   3. Mary, Blessed Virgin, Saint—Devotion to—Mexico.
4. Mexico—Religious life and customs.   5. Church work with Hispanic
Americans.   I. Elizondo, Virgilio P., 1935–   II. Deck, Allan Figueroa, 1945–
III. Matovina, Timothy M., 1955–   IV. Series.
BT660.G8T74   2006
232.91'7097253—dc22   2005025991

Printed in the United States of America

♾ ™ The paper used in this publication meets the minimum requirements of American
National Standard for Information Sciences—Permanence of Paper for Printed Library
Materials, ANSI/NISO Z39.48–1992.

The appearance of Mary to the native Juan Diego on the hill of Tepeyac in 1531 had a decisive effect on evangelization. Its influence greatly overflows the boundaries of Mexico, spreading to the whole continent. America, which historically has been and still is a melting pot of peoples, has recognized in the *mestiza* face of the Virgin of Tepeyac, in Blessed Mary of Guadalupe, an impressive example of a perfectly inculturated evangelization. Consequently, not only in Central and South America, but in North America as well, the Virgin of Guadalupe is venerated as queen of all America.

With the passage of time, pastors and faithful alike have grown increasingly conscious of the role of the Virgin Mary in the evangelization of America. In the prayer composed for the Special Assembly for America of the Synod of Bishops, holy Mary of Guadalupe is invoked as "patroness of all America and star of the first and new evangelization." In view of this, I welcome with joy the proposal of the synod fathers that the feast of Our Lady of Guadalupe, mother and evangelizer of America, be celebrated throughout the continent on December 12. It is my heartfelt hope that she whose intercession was responsible for strengthening the faith of the first disciples (cf. John 2:11) will by her maternal intercession guide the church in America, obtaining the outpouring of the Holy Spirit, as she once did for the early church (cf. Acts 1:14), so that the new evangelization may yield a splendid flowering of Christian life.

Pope John Paul II, Ecclesia in America (1999), #11

Contents

Introduction

Timothy Matovina

Several years ago I attended the 70th wedding anniversary Mass of Doña Manuela and Don José, a couple who had been married in the midst of the Mexican Revolution. The church was packed with friends, relatives, and the couple's children, grandchildren, great-grandchildren, and even two great-great-grandchildren. After communion Doña Manuela rolled her husband in his wheelchair over to a side altar of Our Lady of Guadalupe. Holding his hand and gazing into Guadalupe's eyes, she uttered a prayer in Spanish that she probably intended to be private, but was audible throughout the hushed silence of the congregation seated behind her. "Virgencita linda," she began as she poured out her soul to her celestial mother and thanked Guadalupe for her family and the joys, blessings, and help during hardships over many years. Her lengthy prayer was punctuated with a self-made litany to Guadalupe which included invocations such as "Tú, quien eres la madre de todos [you, who are the mother of all]. . .que nunca nos abandonas [who never abandons us]. . .quien nos acompaña en nuestros dolores [who accompanies us in our sorrows]. . ."

But what I remember most was the touching way Doña Manuela finished her prayer. She told Guadalupe that she had tried to be the best mother she could but that soon she and her husband would not be in this world. Then she passed the mantle of her own motherhood back to Guadalupe: "Yo he sido la madre de esta familia para unos poco años, pero tú eres la madre de todos para siempre. Cuidáles a estos tus hijos cuando Dios ya me llame de este mundo" [I have been the mother of this family for but a few years, but you are the mother of all forever. Care for these your children when God calls me from this world].

Countless devotees like Doña Manuela have long revered Our Lady of Guadalupe as their cherished *madre querida*. At the unanimous request of the bishops of the hemisphere, Pope John Paul II recently affirmed this conviction of the faithful in acclaiming Our Lady of Guadalupe the "mother and evangelizer of America," from Tierra del Fuego to the northernmost reaches of Canada. Noting that Guadalupe is a *mestiza*—a person of mixed race who calls all peoples of the hemisphere to form a united America—Pope John Paul also stated that Guadalupe's image and message present "an impressive example of a perfectly inculturated evangelization" (*Ecclesia in America*, #11). His proclamation further enhanced the growth of Guadalupan devotion, her role in his call for a new evangelization, and her prominence as the most powerful religious image indigenous to the Western Hemisphere. Her basilica in Mexico City is the most visited pilgrimage site on the American continent. Guadalupe continues to appear in the daily lives of her faithful: on home altars, T-shirts, tattoos, murals, parish churches, medals, refrigerator magnets, wall hangings, and in countless conversations and daily prayers. A growing number of Protestants have become attracted to the treasures of Guadalupe and celebrate her December 12 feast. Catholic shrines dedicated to her are located as far north as Johnstown, Cape Breton, Nova Scotia; at least one Canadian bishop has advocated making Guadalupe's feast a holy day of obligation for all Canadian Catholics.

Theologians, pastoral leaders, and devotees themselves have contended for centuries that, though Guadalupe's meaning begins with her maternal love, by no means does it end there. Drawing on the Guadalupe story, image, and devotion as sources for their theological analyses, contemporary Latina and Latino theologians have explored Guadalupe's significance as the premier evangelizer of Mexicans and Mexican Americans, a source of empowerment for women, a symbol of hope and liberation, an inculturated expression of the Christian tradition, a herald of divine election for mission, and a rich resource for theological aesthetics. Theologically, Guadalupe is most frequently associated both with the struggle to overcome the negative effects of the conquest of the Americas and with the hope for a new future of greater justice, faith, reconciliation, harmony, and evangelization amongst all the peoples of the hemisphere. These and other Guadalupan themes are developed in the major contemporary works cited in the select bibliography at the end of this volume.

The most memorable Guadalupan homily I ever heard was from a priest who emphatically challenged congregants with the message "we cannot love Our Lady of Guadalupe unless we love *el pobre* [the poor one] Juan Diego with the commitment of our lives." Like many other homilies and meditations I've heard on Guadalupe, his piercing message tried to illuminate for us, Guadalupe's devotees, the call to discipleship that our devotion and love for her entails. The extent of that love and devotion is a vast reservoir for preachers, directors of religious education, youth ministers, catechists, evangelization teams, spiritual directors, and prayer group leaders to engage the profound Gospel resonances of the Guadalupe event and foster the faith of the multitudes who revere her. This book is a collective effort to help us meet that pastoral challenge. It presents homilies and meditations on Guadalupe from contributors renowned for their pastoral leadership and theological expertise. Enhanced with striking illustrations which are themselves a rich source of contemplating Guadalupe and her message, the volume illuminates the treasure of the Guadalupe tradition for all believers who seek authentic Christian faith more firmly rooted in the native soil of the Americas.

The diversity of contributors and reflections in this volume will enable readers to discover resources for congregations and groups with varying profiles, such as predominantly Mexican, pan-Latino, multicultural, or primarily Euro-American. Several selections are especially suited for preaching within the context of the Eucharist; others are more appropriate for occasions outside of the Eucharist such as a meditation for the *mañanitas* (morning songs) service dedicated to Guadalupe on her feast, a rosary, a retreat, a ministry formation event, or an adult education presentation. But in no instance are the selections intended for direct use; rather they are meant to inspire homilists, catechists, members of the Guadalupanas, teachers, and other leaders to forge presentations on Guadalupe suited for their own communities and contexts.

For Roman Catholics, preaching during the Eucharist takes the form of a homily. Its main features are linking at least one scripture of the day and/or important elements of the liturgical season to the faith life of the worshiping community and to the Eucharist itself. Guadalupe's feast day occurs during the Advent season. In 1754 Pope Benedict XIV established December 12 as the date for her feast; at the request of the Special Assembly for America of the Synod of Bishops, Pope John Paul II declared it an official liturgical feast for all the Americas in 1999. Along with the general option of choosing readings from the Common of the Blessed Virgin Mary, the lectionary used in the United States has specific options for the Gospel and the first reading which are clearly consistent with the Advent theme of joyfully awaiting the Lord's coming: the Annunciation (Luke 1:26–38), the visitation with the first line of the Magnificat (Luke 1:39–47), and Zechariah 2:14–17, which begins "Sing and rejoice, O daughter of Zion! See, I am coming to dwell among you, says the Lord." Several selections in this volume connect the Guadalupe tradition to one or more of these readings, such as those of Allan Figueroa Deck, David García, Jorge Presmanes, and Anastacio Rivera. The second lectionary option for the first reading of the Guadalupe feast presents the "woman clothed with the sun" of Revelation 12 (the assigned text is 11:19a; 12:1–6a, 10ab). First presented in Father Miguel Sánchez's famous 1648 work *Imagen de la Virgen María*, the long tradition of associating Guadalupe with the woman of Revelation 12 is continued in this volume with Mary Doak's selection, which proclaims our call to join this cosmic woman in facing the dragon's fire with faith and the power of the Gospel. Various selections also link Guadalupe to the Advent season, especially that of Rosa María Icaza, which offers a reflection for remembering Guadalupe when her feast falls on the Third Sunday of Advent (as it did in 2004 when she and the other authors prepared their contributions for this volume).

Like numerous homilies and meditations on Guadalupe, most contributors to this volume examine the meanings of the Nahuatl Guadalupe apparition narrative, the *Nican Mopohua* (a title derived from the document's first words, "here we recount"). For proponents of the Guadalupe tradition, the *Nican Mopohua* is the foundational text which recounts the 1531 Guadalupe apparitions to the indigenous neophyte Juan Diego (who was canonized in July 2002 by Pope John Paul II and is commemorated liturgically on December 9). The *Nican Mopohua* narrates how Guadalupe sent Juan Diego to request that Juan de Zumárraga, the first bishop of Mexico, build a temple at Tepeyac in her honor. At first the bishop doubted the celestial origins of this request, but came to believe when Juan Diego presented him exquisite flowers that were out of season and the image of Guadalupe miraculously appeared on the humble *indio*'s *tilma* (cloak). In various ways Guadalupe provided Juan Diego with hope and consolation, including the healing of his uncle, Juan Bernardino. The *Nican Mopohua*'s extensive use of poetic devices, rich imagery, diminutive forms, and the indigenous narrative style of accentuating dialogue has enabled numerous commentators to reflect profoundly on its significance for understanding, living, and announcing the Christian message in the Americas. Their meditations frequently take into account the historical context of sixteenth-century Mesoamerica, especially the tumultuous effects of European conquest on the indigenous peoples.

Contributors to this volume further this long tradition of Guadalupan theological reflection, such as Verónica Méndez's examination of what Guadalupe's command to "erijar un templo" (build a temple) means for Hispanic ministry today and Anita de Luna's analyses of Juan Diego as a model for empowered lay evangelizers and of God's presence and grace in the cultures of conquered peoples. Raymond Brodeur presents his reflection on the Guadalupe apparitions as a personal message addressed to "my dear Juan Diego." These and other presentations in the volume illuminate the evangelizing and catechetical dynamism of the Guadalupe apparition narrative, a sacred text included in the appendix of this volume so that diocesan and parish leaders can engage congregations, adult education groups, young people, retreatants, and other groups in private and collective meditation.

The symbolic meaning of the Guadalupe image itself has also long been a source of fascination and reflection: the angel who holds her aloft, the moon under her feet, the rays of the sun which emanate from behind her, the stars on her mantle, the general color scheme of the icon, her folded hands, downward glance, and compassionate eyes. Guadalupe's daughters and sons constantly revel in her beauty. For numerous devotees the core experience of Guadalupe is the replication of Juan Diego's encounter with their celestial mother: as he did on the hill of Tepeyac, they stand before her. In innumerable conversations, prayers, and sustained gazes at her image, they relive Juan Diego's mystical encounter. What do they see? Numerous commentators have probed this question down through the centuries, an ongoing inquiry continued in this volume through contributions like that of Cecilia González-Andrieu. She explores the theme of beauty in the Guadalupe image and story as a reflection of the Divine Beauty which today beckons us to a greater sense of awe, wonder, gratitude, and faith. Virgilio Elizondo also meditates on the overwhelming experience of beauty in the Guadalupe encounter, which calls all of us to the conversion modeled in the lives of Juan Diego, Juan Bernardino, and Juan de Zumárraga.

Yet another source of reflection on Guadalupe is the prayers and testimonies of her faithful, which began with the construction of the first *ermita* (chapel) dedicated to her on Tepeyac and have expanded ever since. Her litany of achievements, many deemed miracles by her devotees, is endless: providing rain and abundant harvests, driving back flood waters, abating epidemics, safeguarding immigrants, protecting soldiers at war, restoring broken relationships, enabling students to have success in pursuing an education, providing help with employment, healing all manner of infirmity and distress. Prayers of petition and thanksgiving for her intercession flow continuously. In this volume, Jeanette Rodriguez's moving reflection on the "Virgin of the Massacre" engages the courage, faith, and Guadalupan devotion of Mayas in Chiapas, Mexico, as a primary source for her reflection on Guadalupe. Maxwell Johnson takes a wide vista of Guadalupe and her devotees to contend that he and his Lutheran co-religionists can celebrate Guadalupe as one who proclaims the Gospel, embodies God's unmerited grace, and models the path of Christian discipleship in the world.

The broad range of themes outlined here, and many others presented in the selections which follow, is by no means exhaustive. Rather, the sheer variety of insights and convictions in this volume is intended to animate readers to probe more deeply the story, image, devotion, and message of Guadalupe, as well as how the rich Guadalupe tradition, the scriptures, and the spirituality of Advent can mutually enrich one another.

Above all, however, the selections which follow are intended to reveal Guadalupe's fundamental significance as a celestial mother who embodies hope. Her devotees' prime conviction about her is that she never abandons them. As longtime lay leader Socorro Durán puts it in her selection below, for people struggling with illness, poverty, unemployment, inadequate education, a lack of legal status, insecurity, or any kind of discouragement or difficulty, the Guadalupe feast is a needed reminder that "a long time ago Our Lady's apparition to Juan Diego was a sudden, unexpected event which then and now brings hope and expectation to us, the descendants of Juan Diego." In his January 1999 homily at the Basilica of Our Lady of Guadalupe reprinted below to conclude this volume, Pope John Paul II called the church in America the "church of hope" and formally presented the apostolic exhortation *Ecclesia in America* to Guadalupe, "entrusting to the mother and queen of this continent the future of its evangelization." Our hope as collaborators in preparing this collection is that our reflections on the mystery of Guadalupe will deepen our devotion to her, expand our understanding of its Gospel meanings, and inspire us in our calling as the church of America to live the evangelizing message she announces through the Juan Diegos in our midst.

CHAPTER ONE

Facing the Dragon's Fire

Mary Doak

Revelation 12 presents us with one of the most powerful images from this fascinating yet disturbingly violent book. There can be no doubt that an event of cosmic proportions is taking place, since the conflict between the woman and the dragon overwhelms the elemental forces of the universe: the woman is described as clothed with the sun and decorated with the moon and stars, while the dragon dominates the sky and sweeps a third of the stars from the heavens. These are clearly not minor characters, and their importance becomes all the more obvious when we consider that the vision of their momentous struggle in the sky is a central moment in a book describing the battle between good and evil that leads to the ultimate redemption of the world.

We seem to be a long way here from the gentle and compassionate Virgin of Guadalupe, appearing to a humble *campesino* in a colonized land far from the center of the Spanish empire. To be sure, there are obvious similarities of appearance: the Virgin of Guadalupe, like the woman of Revelation, is surrounded by the rays of the sun and outshines the moon at her feet and the stars on her cape. And we are told that the black sash the Virgin wears indicates pregnancy, a condition also shared by the woman of Revelation. Yet the Virgin of Guadalupe's story emphasizes not violent conflict, but compassion, healing, and inclusion. She comes not to further divide people nor oppose them one to another, but to express God's tender mercy for the despised and rejected, for those who have no place among the power players of their day. While the woman of Revelation gives birth in pain and (we must suppose) in great fear of the dragon that threatens her and her child, the Virgin of

1

Guadalupe tells Juan Diego to have no fear, as she will be with him and protect him on his mission to build a more inclusive Church, one that respects the native cultures and peoples rather than vanquishing them.

There are, however, deeper similarities between the appearance of the Virgin of Guadalupe and the vision of the woman of Revelation than may at first be obvious. There is, after all, a "dragon" in Guadalupe's story also, as she comes to Juan Diego shortly after the Spanish empire (then a major world power) had conquered Mexico. The devastating loss of life and destruction of culture by this seemingly unstoppable military power might well have suggested to the indigenous people a strong resemblance between the Spanish conquest of the Americas and the threatening dragon of Revelation, whose powerful tail sweeps a third of the stars from the sky.

There is a further similarity: while the Virgin of Guadalupe shares with the woman of Revelation her stance of opposition to a powerful, life-threatening force, we should remember also that the woman of Revelation is like the Virgin of Guadalupe in sharing the lot of the vulnerable and defenseless, notwithstanding her cosmic power. The woman is, after all, in the process of giving birth while threatened by a dragon ready to tear her child to bits as soon as it comes forth. For all of her power and glory, she is in a truly unenviable position here; she may dominate the sky and overshadow the sun, moon, and stars, but she cannot defend herself or her child. She is bringing forth life against the odds, in the face of an overwhelming force of opposition. Are her birth pangs not a mockery? One would expect that she is suffering this labor for nothing but more heartbreak—until God intervenes to save her child and to protect the woman from the dragon's fury.

We see then that the woman of Revelation is as defenseless and dependent on God as the Virgin of Guadalupe, who comes with no obvious means by which to defend herself or the people with whom she identifies. In the face of the military might of the Spanish empire, Our Lady of Guadalupe appears with her hands clasped in prayer and asking for a house of prayer—she seeks not a military fortress to fight those who threaten us, but a church that will welcome all into a community of self-giving love and prayer! Like the woman of Revelation, the Virgin of Guadalupe depends on God to protect the life she is bringing forth.

In these similarities and differences, both the woman of Revelation and the Virgin of Guadalupe have been rightly recognized as revelations of Mary, the mother of Jesus Christ. Juan Diego identifies the Virgin as Jesus' mother when he reports his vision to the bishop, and church tradition has long interpreted the cosmic woman of Revelation, giving birth to the one who is to rule and doing so in the face of the force of evil, as Mary of Nazareth. All women, of course, risk a great deal in pregnancy and childbirth, but in agreeing to give birth to the future Davidic King according to God's plan, Mary of Nazareth accepted the additional risk of being pregnant as an unmarried woman at a time when this could be punished not merely by social alienation but by stoning to death. Mary willingly took on the task of maternal nurturing that Simeon in the Gospel of Luke rightly foretold would result in her heart being pierced by a sword, as it surely was at Calvary and as is remembered and honored in the many depictions of the mother of Jesus as the Mater Dolorosa. Indeed, some scholars say that Luke's gospel, and especially Mary's prayer, the Magnificat, show Mary willingly accepting a role as the Queen Mother in an alternative government, surely not at all a secure position during the Roman Empire. She is appropriately depicted as giving birth under the most threatening and adverse conditions.

When the Virgin appeared to Juan Diego as an Aztec woman at a time when the Aztec culture was being destroyed and the population decimated, this was thus a continuation of her role as the most faithful disciple who cooperates with God's plan to bring new life to all from among the poor and, at considerable risk to herself, in solidarity with the vulnerable ones. Since God stands with the oppressed and the poor, so too does Mary, the faithful disciple: in her life in Nazareth, in her appearance to Juan Diego, and in the cosmic descriptions of her in the book of Revelation. Our Lady of Guadalupe makes herself vulnerable and takes the part of the vulnerable in the face of overwhelming opposition because she knows well that her task is not to stand on the side of the forces of self-serving power and this-worldly greatness that threaten life, but rather to nurture life against the odds, where it is most in danger from the dragons that would destroy it.

We might recall that the woman of Revelation has been interpreted as symbolizing the Church, which is called to continue making Christ present in the world, and also as representing the Jewish people who brought forth Jesus and the early Christian community under the conditions of Roman oppression. This latter identification may be particularly appropriate, since the Jewish people have nurtured life and sustained community as a threatened people amid oppressive forces for millennia. And of course it has long been a Christian tradition to see Mary, the most faithful disciple, as the model of the Church's vocation and of ideal Christian discipleship. So these various interpretations of the woman of Revelation (as Mary, as the Church, as the Jewish people) all point to the same truth: we Christians are called to join the Jewish people in serving as God's people on earth, and so we must take up the task of nurturing life against the odds, in the face of the destructive dragons that are crouching, ready to destroy all the good we have been given or can achieve. We must trust in God to overcome the powers of evil that we cannot overcome on our own, including the very real, this-worldly forces of oppression. While the vision of the woman of Revelation depicts with clarity the threat under which we fulfill God's will and seek to bring forth and nurture new life, the appearance of the Virgin of Guadalupe also reminds us that placing ourselves in this vulnerable position is a choice that Mary made and asks us to make.

We would do well to reflect for a moment on the fact that, as in so many of our Christian stories, God's message in the story of Guadalupe and in the book of Revelation comes first to the powerless of the world—the threatened, the despised, the seemingly insignificant ones. We have become very familiar with this pattern in our Christian tradition, as so many times in the Bible and in the lives of the saints, it is the poor and the humble (rather than the powerful and the socially or religiously important) who are privileged to receive God in their midst. This pattern is so common that we can forget the simple truth that every time God takes the side of the powerless, there is lurking nearby a threatening dragon whose power is oriented to consuming others. Sometimes, I suspect, we presume that by choosing the poor and powerless, God is standing aside from all human politics and taking no part in the conflicts of this world. After all, those of us who find our place more easily among the powerful than among the insignificant ones tend to think of the poor as simply those outside of the worldly conflicts that are enacted and resolved by the people we recognize as powerful and important. It is easy to overlook the ways in which those who are marginalized bear the effects of the misuse of this-worldly power: being marginal, their suffering is seldom noticed by others, and they die before their time (as Gustavo Gutiérrez emphasizes) with little recognition of their lives or their deaths. As the book of Revelation reminds us, worldly power and security are seldom neutral but rather in so many ways are other-consuming forces directed against the lives of the poor.

The poor, too, often come to see themselves as irrelevant, as Juan Diego indicates in repeatedly protesting that he is unworthy and that it is not his proper role to speak to the Spanish bishop who ruled the Church in Mexico City. Yet it is among these powerless that the Virgin of Guadalupe locates herself (as does the woman of the book of Revelation), revealing again that to God no one is insignificant, no one is irrelevant. Juan Diego is not in her eyes an uneducated and irrelevant man who has no achievements to make him worth remembering in human history. To the contrary, she addresses him as God surely sees him, as a "dignified son," while he recognizes her vulnerability as "the most abandoned of my daughters."

Our passage from the book of Revelation can then lead us to an even deeper appreciation of the appearance of Our Lady of Guadalupe, since Revelation's image of the woman giving birth in the face of a devouring dragon confronts us with the fact that it is never an easy or a safe thing to side with the poor and powerless ones. Our Lady's offer of compassionate love is no cheap grace; it does not come without cost. It was not easy for Mary of Nazareth, it has not been easy for the Jewish people or the Christian churches, and it is not easy now to be a faithful disciple. Discipleship is always exercised in opposition to the dragons of other-consuming power that dominate this world.

The book of Revelation reminds us of the cost of discipleship while also conveying an urgent call: the only locations available in this description of the heavens are either with the dragon or in his line of fire. Yet, against the odds, we learn that all will be resolved with a clear victory for the woman and her children, along with defeat of the dragon. Despite the violent tone, there is good news, Gospel hope, offered here: however powerful evil seems to be now, it will be defeated and in the end the good will triumph. No matter how much the dragons, the powerful forces of aggression and self-assertion, dominate the world in which we are called to be faithful disciples, the good news is that in God's time they will be overcome. Despite all appearances to the contrary, life and love will survive and finally flourish; the self-aggrandizing and other-consuming power that is so often successful in this world will not achieve its end, but will consume itself. The dragon cannot win. We are called to share Mary's trust that God will save the vulnerable life that we cannot secure with our own powers.

However much we need the corrective of the book of Revelation to remind us of the urgency and the cost of the Christian discipleship exemplified by Mary, we also need the story of the appearance of the Virgin to Juan Diego to clarify a central aspect of the Gospel message that may be misplaced amid the stark conflict of the book of Revelation. While the vision of John of Patmos focuses on the opposition between the good that will win and the evil that will lose, the appearance to Juan Diego emphasizes that we are all called to join in the community of self-giving love that will be victorious in the end. As becomes evident in the Virgin's message to the Spanish bishop, the conquerors who have so harshly treated the indigenous people and their culture are not treated harshly in return, but are welcomed into the new community—though on the terms of Christian discipleship, not on the terms of the dragon. That is, they must seek to nurture the life and dignity of the vulnerable, rather than securing their own existence and power. They (and we) are not vilified, but invited in, invited through Mary's message to Juan Diego to receive the good news that God is bringing forth new life among us, in a community that is open to all who will join in this reverence for human life and who are willing to live by other-directed love.

We all, of course, have to acknowledge that we have not always stood with Mary and the many others who have risked their lives to carry on Jesus' redemptive task. We have all found ourselves at times on the side of life-consuming power and aggression. Sometimes we join the dragon willingly, because none of us are immune to the attractions of this-worldly power and its temptation to secure our own existence and importance at the cost of others. But other times, perhaps more commonly, we are merely frightened, hiding behind a dragon we are afraid to challenge or oppose. Still, we are sinners, in what we have done and in what we have failed to do. We have too often served the cause of the dragon and its threat to life, rather than God's project of nurturing life, and we stand in need of God's merciful forgiveness.

But here in the Virgin of Guadalupe's tender message to Juan Diego, the Gospel of forgiveness is generously offered again. We are all invited to join the new community of self-giving love, to see ourselves as the equally beloved and dignified children of God, and to dedicate ourselves to one another. We are forgiven! We too, Guadalupe assures us, are all invited to join this new Church!

The image of Our Lady of Guadalupe has been venerated and deeply cherished for hundreds of years now, especially by those who, like Juan Diego, have been told that they are insignificant, unworthy, and of little value to the powers of this world. Mary's message that the poor, and those who are despised for their culture, skin color, or race, are truly dignified and beloved children of God still comes as an important revelation and source of great joy. However, as the devotion to Our Lady of Guadalupe spreads among those of us who are not poor, who are not Mexican or *mestizo*, and who are not among those treated by society as insignificant, our attention might well focus on the Virgin's loving and forgiving message to the Spanish bishop. We may not be the ones Mary herself identifies with through her dress and skin color in this story, and we may not easily relate to the experiences of the humble Juan Diego. But we have a part in the story nonetheless—among those who inhabit the bishop's palace. We who are accustomed to being treated as significant in this world are also invited into God's new community, as was the bishop and his household, but as we have seen there is a cost to accepting this invitation. We are invited to give up our central position, to move to the margins and allow those our society tells us are the unimportant ones to be in the center of our community's attention and concern. We who are secure in this world are called to take our place among those who are vulnerable and threatened, joining the bishop in his tears of joy and in his repentance at having failed to see the beauty and worth of the lives around us.

There is, then, good news here for all of us. We are all invited in, and we are all included as who we most essentially are. Juan Diego is not asked to give up his native culture but to see God revealed in it; the bishop is not asked to become an indigenous *campesino*, or even to stop being a bishop. Like us, the bishop and his household are invited to join as who they are— provided they are willing to give up being the center, the self-aggrandizing power that threatens other life, and join instead with Mary in Jesus' mission of building a community that nurtures life and cares for the most vulnerable. Mexicans are not asked to deny their Mexican heritage, neither are non-Mexicans asked to adopt Mexican culture or to pretend to be *mestizo*; the Virgin of Guadalupe comes instead with the message that all of us are beloved of God and invited to join God's community. She presents us again with the Gospel message, the good news of redemption, offered freely to liberate us from our sinful selfishness.

Joining Juan Diego and his bishop in building the church Our Lady asks for is not an easy task. This invitation cannot be accepted without risk, especially for those of us who are benefiting from the current situation and who must then give up being the center of importance and refuse to use our energies and resources for self-aggrandizement. We find ourselves negotiating a world of many dragons, as there is no lack of temptation to defend our own position and importance, and there is much power arrayed against those who risk dedicating themselves to sustaining others' lives rather than securing their own. If we are to persist in answering Mary's request that we become a community of the poor and vulnerable in the line of the dragon's fire, we will need God's grace and the help of Mary's other children to recognize and to resist the dragons that threaten life in our context.

Still, however difficult it is and will be, we know that this is where true joy and real security are found. There is liberation for all in this good news: liberation from the burden of self-protection as well as from self-deprecation. God has graciously invited us to serve God's kingdom not by increasing our own importance in this world but by dedicating our energies and resources to building communities that nurture life and privilege the vulnerable. And we know that we have no reason to fear: Our Lady of Guadalupe has promised heaven's protection to us, and the new life we bring forth in the face of threatening dragons will be vindicated by God, as we learn from the book of Revelation. The Virgin's encouragement to Juan Diego speaks across the centuries to all of us today as we struggle to commit ourselves wholeheartedly to the service of God's kingdom: "Am I not here, your mother? Are you not under my shadow and protection? . . . Who else do you need?"

CHAPTER TWO

⌒

Seized and Saturated by Gift: Living for Others

Allan Figueroa Deck, S.J.

The purpose of preaching in the life of the Church is expressed very well in the phrase "the Word was made flesh." Today's readings together with the story of Mary's apparitions at Tepeyac almost five centuries ago stress the fact that God continues to enter into our lives and engage us. God's Word literally became flesh when the Virgin Mary agreed to cooperate with God's plan of redemption. And that Word continues to become flesh in the many responses we make to God's initiatives in our lives. In Luke's gospel today Mary models this response of loving service in her journey of solidarity to her cousin Elizabeth. St. Juan Diego modeled it as well in his response to Guadalupe's request that "a church be built" in the heartland of the Americas.

Good preaching we are told must help people connect the scriptures with their lives, with action. Another way to say that is to say that preaching must motivate. It's not enough to hear the word, to learn the lesson, to merely know our faith. Like Mary and later like Juan Diego we must be moved to act on the faith, to be free enough to truly choose to follow Christ, to live for others just as Jesus did.

The devotion to Our Lady of Guadalupe provides an especially powerful example of the role and importance of symbols in transforming faith into action. The Guadalupe story is a particularly vivid example of how a narrative taps into our human longing for meaning, for a vision of ourselves and

11

of our world. This story's development over time and the continuing response it receives make it very special.

Narratives and symbols play an essential role in every human life. Gerald Arbuckle helps us understand how that is by giving us a simple yet insightful definition: Symbol (and story) is *emotionally experienced meaning*. The Guadalupe story is surely just that. Virgilio Elizondo's writings illustrate the many levels of the symbolic meaning behind the image itself and its power to motivate. The image and apparition narrative had much significance for the Aztecs and other indigenous people. The image functions as a sacred, highly graphic vision of Christianity for the native people in dialogue with their most cherished beliefs. In the Guadalupe story the people of the Americas are challenged to construct the church, to labor in the building of God's Reign on earth. Other commentators have taken the image and projected on it many meanings. This is good and normal for symbols, since they have an inexhaustible potential to help us see, accept, and act on new insights about life's most important concerns.

As a result the Guadalupe phenomenon continues to take on more and more meaning for ever-widening audiences: the Mexican people themselves, the Mexican Americans, U.S. Latinos/as in general, and all those who live in the Americas. César Chávez fittingly interpreted the image of Guadalupe in terms of the farm workers' struggles for justice. Many women today, especially Latinas, appropriately interpret Guadalupe in terms of a new vision of and for women, their dignity, equality, and human rights. The image's growing popularity among Americans of European origin suggests that the Guadalupe narrative also strikes a chord in their own hearts.

Today's gospel highlights a particular meaning that the events at Tepeyac have for Christians. This is what I want to stress today: The story of Tepeyac, like Luke's portrayal of the Annunciation, the Magnificat, and Mary's journey to visit her cousin Elizabeth, graphically portrays the central role of love and service in our Christian lives. Our readings help us grasp today's celebration in ways that reinforce our understanding of Christian identity—in terms of prayer and action, faith and the pursuit of justice, social and ethical concerns, and especially concern for the poor and oppressed. Another way to state this is to say that at the heart of the Christian identity and vocation is the mystery of Incarnation: God is love becoming flesh, concern for others showing itself concretely in action. Mary surely played an essential role in this tremendous mystery. The Guadalupe event brought Christ to the native people of the Americas. So it makes a great deal of sense to be celebrating this Solemnity of Our Lady of Guadalupe during Advent when we turn our hearts and minds to Christ's coming at Christmas and definitively at the end of time.

Yet I want to sound a note of caution. Sometimes our understanding of the Guadalupe story and image lacks balance. Our way of talking about it often fails to stress the importance of action. The Guadalupe tradition can play into an imbalance between passivity and activity, between the courage of accepting God's unconditional love as beautifully expressed by Mary and the courage to act, to reach out to one's neighbor in loving care and service. The second and often neglected part of the Great Commandment tells us to love our neighbor as we do ourselves. Love is about receiving and giving, not just receiving. The image popularly projected of Mary, even of our Lady of Guadalupe, is sometimes simply that of a loving mother who literally lavishes care and concern on her needy children. That is half the story and certainly the most important part of it. Yet the failure to plumb the fuller meaning of Mary for us, for the Church, can lead to romanticizing and sentimentality. What is sometimes left out are precisely the ethical and moral implications of the Guadalupe story: its call to action for all who contemplate its meaning.

The Marian and Guadalupe traditions are dense and complex. The story is about the union of love and power or, better yet, empowerment. Mary calls us to tap into God's power in response to the divine initiatives of love in creating, redeeming, and liberating all humankind. For me, then, it is an urgent task to express the Guadalupe story and our Marian traditions in more balanced ways, ones that do justice to Mary's profound significance. The message of Guadalupe centers on the familiar, simple yet profound idea that Christian discipleship is about responding as Mary did to God's lavish giving of gifts. Love of God and neighbor flows from a deep, personal realization of God's life-giving generosity and faithfulness.

The readings from Luke's gospel remind us that it all begins with God's action. In the Annunciation we hear about the initiative God took in selecting Mary of Nazareth to be the Mother of our Savior. Her own responses are found in words and deeds: the strong, stunning language of the Magnificat ("He puts the mighty down from their thrones . . ." Luke 1:52) and the hard journey to be of assistance to her cousin Elizabeth. Scripture scholars tell us that the image of the Holy Spirit at work in the Annunciation evokes the Spirit's work at the beginning of time at creation itself. The Annunciation also evokes God's creative love: God renews fallen humanity and we enter anew into the Garden of God's friendship, the wonderful gift from which we alienate ourselves through sin. Today's gospel reminds us that beyond creation and redemption, God's love is manifested in liberating action like Mary's initiative to serve her cousin in her hour of need. The dramatic encounter between Mary and Elizabeth reveals Mary as a real—even tough—woman of action. She connects love of God with love of neighbor. This love is not only concerned with kindness but also with justice, and from it flows the *transformation* of the concrete conditions that oppress us. Mary, then, witnesses to the essential connection between Christian faith and justice. God's presence in the midst of the loving encounter of concern and service is felt even *viscerally*. Elizabeth tells us that the child in her womb literally leapt!

In the Old Testament we are reminded of the initiative God took with Israel, especially the Covenant and God's promise of care for the materially poor. We hear the covenant relationship between Yahweh and Israel described as a passionate love affair. At this time of Advent we are also reminded about the endurance of God's gift of life, the reliability of God's promise. The book of Revelation portrays the coming fulfillment of God's promises at the end of time when the justice of God's Reign will forever triumph (11:19). Indeed, today in our Eucharist we experience anew the gracious gift-giving of God through sacramental signs and wonders. They give us a magnificent vision of things to come and, like Mary in today's gospel, they invite us to contemplate God's mighty deeds in real time.

So the story of Our Lady of Guadalupe is about this same divine initiative at the dawn of the Americas in the geographic bridge between the two Americas that is called Mexico. The first Christians of the New World are given a tangible expression of God's inexhaustible love in a form *uniquely suited to them*. Mary, the Mother of God, is said to appear to St. Juan Diego, to engage in a lively dialogue with him in his native tongue and, in turn, elicit from him a generous response. He is asked to have a temple built on that place where the living God of Jesus Christ might be known and served. He is challenged to not only stand in awe and amazement before the beautiful person of Jesus' Mother, but also to act on behalf of others, his community. He *contemplates* the vision of God in and through the Guadalupan apparition and he *acts* in response, at first hesitatingly but eventually wholeheartedly.

Yes, the love of God and neighbor for us Christians must always spring from the prior experience of *God's love for us*. This is fundamental. For us the way of faith is not the result of rational conclusions or ideologies. The way of faith begins with personal and communal experience, with loving dialogue and the felt realization of how God has acted first, how God has *loved first*.

That love is pure gift and the faith that wells up in its wake is itself more gift. Theologian Michael Downey explains:

> . . . the gift is always and everywhere an offer. One who has learned to receive the gift is contemplative, as is one who lives freely and responsibly with, in and from the gift. Contemplation is a way of beholding in wonder and in gratitude the presence of God in human life, history, the world, and the Church. Whether at prayer or immersed in activity, the contemplative is *seized and saturated by gift*. (Quoted in Joseph F. Conwell, S.J., *Walking in the Spirit*, p. vii.)

The utter gratuity of God's offer of love as reflected so powerfully in the Gospel and in the Guadalupe story is often not grasped in its deeper meaning for us. Our failure to grasp the meaning of today's Gospel originates perhaps from the gnawing sense of unworthiness that afflicts us humans on the one hand and our striving to make ourselves worthy by our own efforts on the other. The scriptures tell us, in contrast, to simply accept our worthiness as a gift. One of the most difficult things for us human beings is the courage to accept God's acceptance. No matter how much we have performed, succeeded, or lived up to the expectations of others, for so many of us, there is never enough acceptance.

A recent biography of the great spiritual writer Henri Nouwen illustrates how someone as gifted as Father Nouwen suffered terribly all his life from a feeling of inacceptability and unworthiness. Nouwen poignantly tells us about the spiritual breakthrough he experienced at L'Hermitage in St. Petersburg, Russia, as he contemplated Rembrandt's *Return of the Prodigal Son*. Nouwen suffered from an irrational sense of being rejected by his father. Rembrandt's painting helped him discover the meaning of the Gospel of the Prodigal Son and apply it to himself.

Our U.S. culture often proposes a false solution to our human quest for worthiness and meaning, a solution that runs contrary to the Gospel and the message of Guadalupe. I would argue that this mistaken idea is very prevalent today in our country. With all the good intentions in the world, we raise our children to "justify their existence," to make something of themselves, succeed and triumph in life. We propose to them that they do this by obeying God's laws, fulfilling their responsibilities and generally "being good." They can thus make themselves acceptable to God! The danger of this way of looking at life is found in the fact that there is some truth to it. Yes, we need to be responsible people! But the heart of the Christian message we see in today's gospel and in the Guadalupe message is that God's love is unconditional, pure gift. Much worry and stress come about as a result of our culture's emphasis on individual performance and competition with others. While this orientation is especially strong in U.S. culture, it has never been totally lacking in Latino cultures and may be growing in influence among them as Latinos engage the U.S. cultural mainstream.

The image of the Madonna of Guadalupe, however, is a countercultural stroke in a very different direction. Its message is about God's creative initiative as the alpha and the omega, the *starting and the end points*, for all life in the universe and for all being itself. In the United States today this message is more needed than ever. People are so often locked in the jails of self-justification, self-promotion, upward mobility, wealth, and power in a mad race toward "success." For the most part, accordingly, God's grace has little or nothing to do with most of our life's activities. Those activities depend on one's own talent, energy, and worthiness, even on one's hereditary genes, and not on God. We are basically loners on the earth caught in a competitive race toward an elusive "top." This sad and destructive mentality saps the life out of so many people today.

The Guadalupe story points to a deeply Christian spirituality of contemplative action in which God's people are permeated with a sense of God's lavish love. Mary's spirituality was deeply biblical. For her it always was about what God does and her generous response to that unspeakable love. Filled with the vitality that comes only from a deep and lasting love, God's people like Mary respond in kind, that is, with love and care for others. Mary of Guadalupe is an icon that transforms and energizes us as we contemplate it. We have God's approval *now* and really are helpless to do anything to gain it. God just gives it, period. This is the story, to use St. Augustine's term, of God's *prevenient grace*. First and foremost, then, life is not a matter of what one does or does not do; it is about *what God has done and is doing*. Contrary to what so many Christians seemingly think, it is not that we do good and are rewarded for it, but rather that God does good and we respond in gratitude.

The figure of Mary reaching out in service as a woman of action represents the balance needed in life whereby our human efforts are always grounded not in our own resources but in God's inexhaustible grace. When people are loved, supported, and personally called, they respond in kind to others. The story of Our Lady of Guadalupe is one of care and concern for the marginalized and forgotten of this world. It is a story of tender love mingled with stirring challenges to move beyond the inertia of fear. St. Juan Diego's story is a beautiful example of how a doubtful and fearful man gained confidence through his dialogue with and contemplation of Mary of Guadalupe. The church he asked to have built was not so much one of brick and mortar, but rather the People of God, the Church of the Americas, of which we here in the United States are a part.

In the Eucharist, just as in the Annunciation and Guadalupe stories, Christ becomes flesh for us. Christ is embodied in the historical Jesus conceived at the Annunciation. Christ is embodied in the community of faith, the Church, that Mary symbolizes more than anyone. She was the first to respond to God's loving initiative and, beyond anyone's wildest dreams, she was fruitful. Mary brings Christ to others just as Christ is brought here to us today in this Eucharistic liturgy and as we, in turn, bring Christ to others as we leave this celebration today.

Seized and saturated by such love, what will be our response to others, especially to those most in need? Through the saving power of God we have all become servants of the Word. This is done in many different ways but especially by how we use our financial resources, advocate for the voiceless in our society, and seek to empower the powerless. Like Mary of Guadalupe let us nurture and embody that Word in our hearts, make it flesh in our awareness and faithful response of service to others. The symbol of Guadalupe places our response to the challenges of the world within the context of a human history touched by grace. It provides a powerfully motivating example of what it means to live for others and not just for oneself. This tradition provides powerful motivations for you and me to journey with renewed energy and conviction along the path of Christian prophetic witness in the footsteps of Mary, the first Christian, the first follower of Jesus Christ.

CHAPTER THREE

You Can Do It

David García

When we were young and were confronted with something that was difficult to do, how many times did we say to ourselves or others, "I can't do this. It is too much. I will never be able."

Who was the one that was most often there to gently let us know that we could do it, that it was possible, and that she would be there to help and guide and support us?

Our mother.

Through each challenge, each moment that called us to do more, our mother coaxed us through it and helped us realize that we could always do more than we ever thought possible. Maybe it was to take that first step, or to get through the first day in school, or to learn a musical instrument, or to first ride a bicycle. We said, "I can't do it, not me" and she said, "You can."

Juan Diego said the same thing to La Virgen de Guadalupe when she asked him to be her messenger. He can't do it. He shouldn't do it. He is not one of the great or important persons to take such a message from the Mother of God to the bishop. Why in the world would she choose someone like him, a nobody, a scum? There are so many others who could do what she wants, who could represent her with dignity. He is simply not good enough. He is not worthy. So goes Juan Diego's response to Guadalupe when at first the bishop doesn't believe him.

But his mother Guadalupe is insistent that he can do it. He is the one to take her message. He is to be the messenger of God to the powers that be. In this she is simply following in the long line of stories in Scripture showing that God intervenes on the part of the little ones, on the part of the

19

suffering, the oppressed, and those who cry out for justice. And, not only does God intervene for them, but God uses them to do the works of God. God sends especially the powerless to confront the powerful. Despite the seeming nothingness of those messengers, God does great things. God's power shows in the powerlessness of the ones called. As St. Paul says, "God uses the meek to confound the proud" (1 Cor. 1:27–28).

Guadalupe responds to Juan Diego's protests of unworthiness. She affirms that Juan Diego is the least of her children. However, she insists that it is precisely because he is among the least that she favors him. It is precisely because he is among the conquered, the dispossessed, that he is chosen to take the message to those with power, to the conquerors. She will show through the conquered that it is God who conquers.

We did it as young people with our mother. Juan Diego did it as a seemingly insignificant person with his mother. "I can't do it. I am not good enough." "Yes, you can do it. Yes, you are good enough."

In the gospel we read for this feast, the gospel of the Annunciation (Luke 1:26–38), Mary is no stranger to this reversal of roles. She herself was the least likely to be selected as the mother of God. Coming from Nazareth, a marginal area of Judaism, one where other people of different races and religious beliefs freely mixed with the local population, she had no particular upbringing or status that would single her out for such a great privilege. The angel who comes to tell her that God wants her for a special task disturbs her by his very greeting. The messenger tells her she is favored by God. It is not Moses or one of the prophets receiving this greeting, but a lowly young woman, completely different from what one would expect.

Mary's inquiry as to how the angel's words will come to pass does not show a lack of faith, but rather an overwhelming sense of littleness in the face of such a great request, of not comprehending how in the world God could choose such a person as herself. The angel makes it clear that God knows what is going to happen and has chosen her to participate in the plan of salvation. Mary's simple yet profound acceptance, "let it be done," models for us what it means to be a faithful disciple, to hear the Word of God and allow it to dwell within so that it can become a reality.

The gospel passage that follows this one is about another woman feeling unworthy (Luke 1:39–47). Elizabeth, the cousin of Mary, shouts out a greeting as Mary enters her home, "How am I worthy that the mother of my Lord should come to me?" In her own feeling of inadequacy, Elizabeth blesses her cousin Mary, affirming Mary's choice to hear the word and follow it. She says, "Blessed are you who believe what the Lord has promised will be fulfilled." Elizabeth has also been called and has opted to be a messenger and servant of God in the plan of salvation by receiving Mary, announcing words of faith, and bearing John the Baptist, who would imitate his mother in later announcing the time of God's fulfillment.

Both women are seen as unworthy in the eyes of the people of their time, yet both are essential to the plan of God to bring salvation, to proclaim the Good News of God's great goodness to all.

Juan Diego stands in this long line of divine surprises: the grace-filled presence and action of a God who chooses those who no one expects to be the main messengers of the Good News. Juan Diego at first resists, but his mother Guadalupe assures him that he is the one who will do it and make a new thing happen. He can do it. She will help him.

We are the Juan Diegos of today. How often have we felt we can't do it. We put ourselves down. We think we are not good enough. Sometimes others tell us in subtle or not so subtle ways that we are not good enough. Some of us grow up with those kinds of words in our ears all the time, from school to home to neighborhood to work. You are not good, you are poor, you are uneducated, you come from that side of town, you don't speak that well, your family is not important, you are nobody.

Yet we are also called as Juan Diego was called. It is time to hear the voice of our mother in our ears. "You can do it." God chooses the little ones to do the great things in history. For God nothing is impossible. Our vocation, our calling, is also to create something new in the Church. It is to transform the Church by building not a temple, but a people, a people who transform the community, the society, and the world. It is a people who speak and live that compassion which Mary of Guadalupe wants to show through her temple in Tepeyac. It is a people who speak and live that justice for the poor. It is a people who speak for those who have been belittled. It is a people who speak for those left out. It is a people who speak for those put down by others and by society.

Juan Diego in the end accomplishes the mission that Guadalupe gives him. The result is something he never imagined possible.

God can do all things. For God nothing is impossible.

Juan Diego was not canonized a saint for over 470 years. Many thought it might never happen, yet for millions over those years he was always a saint. His story has always appealed to those who have said, "I can't do it." Maybe the fact that he was recently canonized a saint has helped us all to reacquaint ourselves with this simple yet profound figure of faith. Maybe waiting all these centuries for the official recognition simply adds to the story of the insignificant *indio* and makes it a story not only for then but for now. The waiting is part of what powerless and little people always must do. The waiting is what Mary did after saying yes. The waiting is what Elizabeth did. The waiting is what we often do while we live out our yes to God's call. The faithful waiting can actually bring the new life that we need to answer the call of God. The waiting is not passive; it is an active struggle for faith, compassion, and justice, but always with the sure hope that those who wait upon the Lord do not wait in vain.

Juan Diego's story is our story. His hesitancy is ours in the face of being called to share the Good News and change our world. His feelings of nothingness are reflected in our sense of inadequacy against a society that puts us down at every turn. His call to take the message is our call to tell others that God wants things different, that God loves those who are poor and powerless, that God does not forget the sufferings of God's people, and that God is with us on our pilgrimage through a hostile world.

Juan Diego in his hesitancy and feelings of inadequacy speaks to us of the reality of being imperfect people in an imperfect world. It is the story of faith in the face of this challenge. It is faith in a God who does not forget us in our sufferings, and in the everyday struggles to live fully and do the things that can make a difference in our lives and the lives of those around us. It is a faith in the God who created us and who has given us all we need to do His work while we are here in this world. It is faith in a God who also called a young woman to do great and marvelous things. That woman is the one we now call Mary, our mother.

Our mother is telling us we can do it; we can make a difference in the world. We can be different if we believe in ourselves as she believes in us. She is behind us. She is coaxing us. She is giving us a reason to believe in ourselves. She is saying, "Think great thoughts. Have a great vision of the way things can be, and do the great things needed to help the world get there."

As we go through life, we remember what our own mother told us as children. We carry much of her thoughts, much of her values, much of her way of looking at the world with us. We feel her presence in us at times when we confront a difficult decision, a tragedy, a crisis, a new challenge. The thoughts of her inside us often give us the strength to do what we don't believe we can do. The thoughts of her inside us guide us to do the right thing when facing a choice.

Guadalupe is our mother. And there is something of our mother in all of us.

CHAPTER FOUR

~

Go Forward in Hope for the Promises of the Lord Will Be Fulfilled

Jorge Presmanes, O.P.

Georgia is one of those states that deny immigrants who are undocumented a driver's license. A couple of years ago I did a lay leadership workshop in that state for the Hispanic community in a sleepy little town not too far from the Florida border. It was there that I met Doña Inez, a woman of hope. She is the mother of five and wife of Don Rodrigo. On Sunday afternoon, we concluded the workshop with the celebration of the Eucharist. The gospel reading was taken from the first chapter of Luke, the narrative of Mary's visitation to Elizabeth, the same gospel reading proclaimed in our liturgy today.

After Mass, warm good-byes were shared and everyone went home. On their way, a nightmare began to unfold as they encountered a series of roadblocks on every street that led out of the church. Don Rodrigo was arrested that night for driving without a license. Everyone in the community knew that what had happened before would now happen again. Men were arrested, the Immigration and Naturalization Service was summoned, and deportation was almost inevitable.

In the immediate aftermath, many of the families of those arrested began to walk back to the church. Fear and hopelessness took hold of those who had gathered. Despair, the fruit of the injustice they had experienced, grew with every second that passed. Breaking the paralysis which had quickly and forcefully descended on the community, Doña Inez stood up and echoed the words of the gospel: "Bendito son los que creen que se cumplirán las promesas del Señor" (Blessed are they who believe that the promises of the Lord will be fulfilled). With these hope-filled words, she knelt before the image of Guadalupe and led us in praying the rosary.

Hope. In its most basic sense, hope is what enables the human person to continue on his or her life's journey. It gives us the will to live and persevere in life. It is hope that allows us to believe that life is worthwhile. Without hope life is desolate, the future is rendered dark and bleak, and in the anguish of despair life is converted into unbearable pain. So was the experience of the Amerindian peoples at the time of the conquest. Their suffering was of a magnitude that it is almost impossible for most today to understand. Theirs was the pain of slavery and of rape. Theirs was the pain of being stripped of land and of faith. The hopelessness and despair that ensued from their conquest led some to the expression of complete dissolution and ruin: suicide.

At that moment in history, when unthinkable suffering was being inflicted on the native peoples of the Americas by our own ancestors, an extraordinary messenger of God's hope was sent. Guadalupe appears to people who had been defeated by a violent and unscrupulous conquest. She appears to the hopeless with a message of hope: I am with you for God hears the cry of the poor; fear not for I will give birth to a son who will bring light to the darkness of the world.

Guadalupe's message of hope was not limited to a specific time and place and moment in history; her message is eternal. And so, led by Doña Inez on that night in south Georgia we knelt before Guadalupe because for almost five hundred years her message of hope has sustained millions upon millions of people who know suffering all too well.

For many, hope is "wishful thinking," but this is not the hope expressed by Guadalupe on Tepeyac nor by Doña Inez on that frightful night in south Georgia. Theirs is a biblical hope whose foundation lies in God's covenant with God's people, the divine promise that God will never abandon us, God's children. Biblical hope, authentic hope, can only be grounded in God and rooted in expectant faith. If our hope is not rooted in God's loving commitment to us, God's children, then our desperate attempt to attain it by our own means will most assuredly be pointless and ineffectual.

For Christians, hope is that conviction, felt deep in our bones and in our spirits, that God is good and that God's promises will be fulfilled. For St. Paul it is the certainty that the future will be blessed by the loving presence of the Spirit (Rom. 8:23–25). Hope, for him, does not exempt us from suffering. On the contrary, hope is born of patient endurance in the midst of suffering (Rom. 5:2–5). Hope is the source of the courage that allows us to walk with

Jesus to the cross with the blessed assurance of the resurrection, of the coming of the Kingdom. Such is the hope that enabled Doña Inez to persevere.

While Christian hope grants extraordinary solace, comfort, and strength to continue on life's journey, it also makes demands. It demands that we trust in the goodness of God and that it be shared with others to whom we have been sent to bring glad tidings. Such was the instruction that Guadalupe gave Juan Diego to go to the bishop and tell him what she had said. But the proclamation of hope cannot be limited to a pronouncement in word alone. It must be proclaimed in word and in deed. It must be manifested in a profound love that becomes the source of hope for others. Hope becomes hope only when we engage in hopeful acts with and for others, for to hoard hope is to destroy hope.

It is not a coincidence that in I Corinthians, Paul places hope between faith and love. Hope, says St. Thomas, is the virtue that enables the Christian to move from faith to love (*Summa*, II.II.17.1). In other words, hope is the fruit of faith and love is the fruit of hope and it is through love expressed in mercy that the reign of God is born. Guadalupe's message of hope is thus also a challenge for the Christian: the challenge to love, the challenge to be compassionate and just.

On a December morning, as Juan Diego walked to attend Mass, Guadalupe began a pilgrimage of hope in loving solidarity with us, God's people. Guadalupe's decision to walk with us on our eschatological pilgrimage teaches us that, oftentimes, the love that is born of hope is expressed simply in an act of solidarity, in being with those who suffer, in walking together with our eyes set firmly on the Kingdom. In his book, *Moral Wisdom*, James Keenan illustrates this very point by recalling an extraordinary gesture of hope-filled love and solidarity. After Christmas Mass in the first year of his papacy, Pope John XXIII left St. Peter's Basilica and went to visit the prisoners at Regina Coeli. He stood before the inmates and said, "You could not come to see me so I have come to see you." The unexpected act of compassion is recorded on the front doors of St. Peter's today. On the bronze panel the sculptor depicts the Holy Father stretching his hands through the prison bars and taking hold of the inmates' hands as he calls them his brothers.

On Tepeyac God stretched out his arms and offered his hand in solidarity to his defeated and suffering children through Guadalupe. In her visitation to Juan Diego, God reached through the barriers of their imprisonment to give hope to the hopeless. Today, God through Guadalupe stretches his arms of hope to us once again. But as Christians we know that the hope granted us calls us to go and do likewise: to love, to be compassionate, to be just, to be generous, to care for the sick, to feed the hungry, to house the homeless, to build the reign of God. As we gather around this altar of hope and feast on God's love we pray through the intercession of *La Guadalupana* that, like her, like blessed John XXIII, and like Doña Inez, we may stretch out our hands to those who suffer so that together we move forward—not naively about the world's suffering or the evil we can inflict on one another—but in solidarity as a people who rest in and are guided by the blessed assurance that the promises of the Lord will be fulfilled.

~

CHAPTER FIVE

Building Bridges as Worlds Collide

Anastacio Rivera, S.J.

Mary, the young maiden of Nazareth, holds a pivotal role in the developing story of humanity in quest of its destiny. In many diverse ways she has been present at critical points in the human epic, but most especially during the birth of Jesus and the conquest of the Americas.

First came that very ordinary day at her home in Nazareth where she went about her household chores as she happily thought about the approaching day of her marriage to Joseph. The formal discussions between their two families had gone well, and soon she and Joseph would be able to celebrate the beginning of their life together as a family.

Suddenly, a bright figure stood before her, cutting through her wedding daydreams and saying to her, "Hail, favored one! The Lord is with you" (Luke 1:28). Mary was stunned; she was barely able to breathe as she tried to make sense of what was happening to her. The angelic figure then said to her, "Do not be afraid, Mary, for you have found favor with God. Behold, you will conceive in your womb and bear a son, and you shall name him Jesus. He will be great and will be called Son of the Most High, and the Lord God will give him the throne of David his father, and he will rule over the house of Jacob forever, and of his kingdom there will be no end" (Luke 1:30–33).

Each word and phrase she was hearing seemed to intensify the shock pounding at Mary. A messenger from God! Favor with God! She is to bear a son! One who will be called Son of the Most High! Throne of David! Rule the house of Jacob! Forever!

Centuries of the religious history of her people flooded over her. Clearly, she was being called to become a strategic player in some vast drama of the

Divine. But how could this be? Why her? And what about Joseph? What about their wedding plans? Finally she gasped in reply: "How can this be, since I have no relations with a man?" (Luke 1:34).

If anything, the answer she received brought still more startling news: "The Holy Spirit will come upon you, and the power of the Most High will overshadow you. Therefore the child to be born will be called holy, the Son of God" (Luke 1:35).

Wonder, litanies of questions, fear, awe, and many more powerful reactions surged through Mary. Her entire universe seemed to be spinning and tilting around in endlessly changing patterns. For all she knew, Mary was being asked to forfeit all the happy plans she and Joseph had been crafting together. Their shared religious tradition made it quite clear that Joseph could not remain faithful to his religion and at the same time accept her in the context of her pregnancy out of wedlock. The world she and Joseph had been creating was on a collision course with the world into which God was inviting her.

Yet that same religious tradition gave her an overwhelming conviction that she was called to be the instrument of God's will. One strong, solid focal point seemed to emerge: have faith in the Lord God. With every last ounce of strength she clung to that one anchor of reality and replied, "Behold, I am the handmaid of the Lord. May it be done to me according to your word" (Luke 1:38).

In faith Mary took her stand. As a result, "The Word became flesh and made his dwelling among us, and we saw his glory, the glory as of the Father's only Son, full of grace and truth" (John 1:14).

Thus a new bridge of intimate relationship sprang up between God and humanity. "In this way the love of God was revealed to us: God sent his only Son into the world so that we might have life through him. In this is love: not that we have loved God, but that he loved us and sent his Son as expiation for our sins" (1 John 4:9–10).

Two worlds—the divine and the human—collided. Instead of cataclysm and annihilation there followed an explosion of redemptive love. Mary herself sang: "My soul proclaims the greatness of the Lord; my spirit rejoices in God my savior. For he has looked upon his handmaid's lowliness; behold, from now on will all ages call me blessed. The Mighty One has done great things for me, and holy is his name" (Luke 1:46–49).

Mary, the woman of Nazareth, through her faith, trust, and love became one of the principal architects of the cosmic bridge between heaven and earth.

Fifteen centuries passed and then came another critical point in the human story. The voyage of discovery by Christopher Columbus brought the two hemispheres of the earth into contact with each other. Suddenly, two very different social-economic-philosophical-religious universes collided. The first, tentative gestures of mutual hospitality gave way to the power tactics in which the stronger European arrivals conquered the weaker indigenous peoples. The conquest became a destructive rampage to wipe out every vestige of the indigenous civilization in the name of Jesus Christ, the Son of Mary. Inevitably the process of evangelization became identified with the rampage of the conquistadores. For the most part the indigenous peoples' profession of belief in the Christian God was no more than a desperate effort to survive.

Finally, after ten years of this tragedy, there came a dark predawn December morning to the hill of Tepeyac on the outskirts of what is now known as Mexico City. Juan Diego, one of the very few natives who had made a true conversion to Christianity, made his way along the slope of Tepeyac and headed for morning Mass at a church several miles down the road. Suddenly he was surrounded by an incredible chorus of birdsong. Juan Diego was stunned; he said to himself: "Where am I? Where do I find myself? Is it possible that I am in the place our ancient ancestors, our grandparents, told about, in the land of flowers, in the land of corn, of our flesh, of our sustenance, possibly in the land of heaven?"

Then the singing stopped and he heard someone calling out to him. "Juan, dearest Juan Diego, sir." Joy enveloped his heart and he started to climb the hill to see who was calling him. When he reached the top of the hill he found an incredibly beautiful lady waiting for him. Everything about her reminded him of some of the most artistically beautiful things he had once known in his Nahuatl culture. Her clothing seemed to radiate with rays of light. The stone on which she stood glittered with light. Even the ground around her shone like a brilliant rainbow. The mounds of thorny cactus and brush were transformed into glittering emeralds. Her voice carried a warm tone of kindness and acceptance.

Then she spoke to him in his own Nahuatl tongue: "Listen *xocoyouh* [my dearest little son], Juan, sir. Where are you going?" With those two short phrases she pronounced a detailed analysis of how she saw him. Normally *xocoyouh* was a term applied to a child to indicate he or she was the last-born child in the family. But Juan Diego was a grown man. In such a context, *xocoyouh* pointed to the downtrodden, helpless condition of the man. The lady does not beat around the bush; she recognizes him as a member of a conquered, devastated people. Yet she also calls him "sir," using the –*tzin* ending applied only to the very important nobles or divinities in his culture. So in the first short phrase she refers directly both to his desperate social status and to the respect and esteem with which she comes to him. Given that double-edged first phrase, her ensuing question, "Where are you going?" takes on a much more radical meaning: What is to become of you and your people?

Juan Diego's response to the question is limited to his immediate errand of going to Mexico-Tlatelolco, "to follow the things of God . . . that are taught to us by the ones who are the images of Our Lord: our priests."

The lady goes on to reveal her reasons for being there: she is the Virgin Mary, Mother of the one true God, and she has come to make her Son manifest to all the people. Indeed, she is also Juan Diego's mother, and the mother of all the people; she has come to help and comfort them in their trials. Then she explains that in order for her to accomplish her mission she needs Juan Diego to go to the bishop of Mexico City and tell him he must build a temple for her on Tepeyac hill.

Juan Diego is quick to understand the enormous significance of what he has just heard. The beautiful lady has clearly identified herself as Mary the mother of the Christian God whom he is just getting to know. But in describing her maternity she has also clearly used specific titles straight from Juan Diego's own previous Nahuatl religious world: "God of Great Truth, the One Through Whom We Live, the Creator of People, the Owner of What Is Close to Us, the Lord of Heaven and Earth, the Provider." Thus she has synthesized into one central concept the "Supreme Being" from two different religious worlds.

The focus of her mission is on that Supreme Being, but she also proclaimed herself the mother of all the inhabitants of the land. "I am truly your compassionate mother, yours and of all the people who live together in this land, and of all the other people of different ancestries, my lovers, those who cry to me, those who seek me, those who trust in me." So she has not only united the two distinct religious worlds, she has also brought all peoples into one common family, her family. She has revealed herself as a unifying bridge.

Juan Diego accepted the mission and immediately set out for the bishop's residence in Mexico City. The dramatic encounter with the lady has so inspired him that he almost forgets that he is now walking into the incredible role of messenger and mediator at quite a rarified level of society. He himself is becoming a bridge.

It does not take long for the bishop and his servants to bring Juan Diego back down to reality. He is dismissed with instructions to come back again some other time so the bishop can more carefully listen to him.

Juan Diego is crushed. Once again his "xocoyouh" reality lands on him in all its brute force. What had he been thinking? How could he have thought anyone would listen to a nobody like him! When he saw the lady he threw himself at her feet and lamented that he is a nobody who will never be believed and therefore it would be better if she would select someone else, one of the truly important people, to carry her message.

Although the Virgin acknowledged that she did indeed have many other people she could have selected for the task, she was not about to let Juan Diego off so easily. She made it quite clear that he was the appointed messenger and tells him firmly to get back to the task of delivering her message.

Juan Diego remained faithful to his task. On the following day he again went through the tedious process of walking back to the bishop's residence, struggled to be allowed entry, and again endured the frustration that despite a detailed interrogation the bishop did not believe him. In fact, this time the bishop added a further admonition. Juan Diego must bring the bishop some sign from the Queen of Heaven.

Upon Juan Diego's report to the Virgin she agreed that on the following day she would give Juan Diego a sign by which the bishop would be finally convinced of the authenticity of Juan Diego's message.

The triumphant encounter promised for the following day did not take place. Juan Diego was unable to return to Tepeyac hill because his uncle, Juan Bernardino, suddenly became ill to the point of death. The only recourse left was to get a priest from Tlatelolco so the uncle might prepare his soul for death.

However, going to Tlatelolco presented a problem; to get there, Juan Diego would have to walk past Tepeyac and the Virgin might well intercept him and interrupt his mission of mercy. What was Juan Diego to do? Obey the Virgin, or help his uncle? He decided the uncle must remain his priority. So he cautiously took a wide detour around the Tepeyac path, only to find that the Virgin still caught up with him. Embarrassed by his delay and evasive efforts, Juan Diego tried to explain. She reassured him that he must not let anything discourage him and that his uncle had already been cured. Juan Diego was comforted by her words and promptly begged her to put him back to work on her mission. She sent him up to the top of Tepeyac to gather the beautiful flowers he would find there. It seemed an impossible task, for Tepeyac was a barren pile of rock and cactus, and at that time of year the freezing temperatures would have killed any vegetation. But Juan Diego promptly obeyed.

At the top of Tepeyac, he was astonished to discover a garden of beautifully blooming flowers. As instructed, he gathered them up into his cloak and returned to the lady. She told him that the flowers were the sign he must take to the bishop.

Thus, Juan Diego is finally able to return to the bishop carrying the precious sign. After another difficult encounter with the servants he was finally allowed to see the bishop. Carefully he detailed his latest encounter with the lady. Following her instructions Juan Diego was now ready to give the bishop the sign he had requested in order to build the church. Moreover, the bishop would thus also finally have proof that the native messenger was speaking the truth. Juan Diego then opened his cloak to present the flowers to the bishop; as the flowers tumbled to the floor the image of the Virgin of Guadalupe miraculously appeared on the robe.

The beautiful lady, who herself had long before been called to become a bridge between heaven and earth, had thus called the conquered indigenous neophyte to become the messenger and instrument by which her Son, the cosmic bridge builder, would bind two worlds together.

As the bridge was built the *xocoyouh* received the gift of sensing anew his own dignity and worth. In simple, direct terms he told the bishop, "You should see the sign that you were asking for in order to carry out her beloved will, and so that it will be clear that my word, my message, is true."

Juan Diego had seen his world despised and nearly destroyed, his people no more than faceless, helpless, and voiceless *xocoyouhs*. Through Mary, the beautiful Virgin of Guadalupe, the hand of God reached into the very heart of Juan Diego to restore the triple flame of faith, hope, and love. Or, in the words of the prophet Isaiah: "Rise up in splendor! Your light has come, the glory of the Lord shines upon you. See, darkness covers the earth, and thick clouds cover the peoples. But upon you the Lord shines, and over you appears his glory" (60:1–2).

The message of Guadalupe endures as the promise to us that the light and glory of God will continue to shine over us as we walk forth into the world of the twenty-first century, a world heavily burdened with multiple challenges. Many new bridges will have to be built.

~

CHAPTER SIX

Who Can Help Us Better to Prepare for Christmas?

Rosa María Icaza, C.C.V.I.

Advent is a season the Church offers us to prepare for the coming of Our Lord Jesus at Christmas, when we commemorate with great joy and gratitude an event that changed history forever, the birth of a baby who is both God and human. Yet, we are also invited to prepare for the second coming of Jesus at the end of the world. So, we are called to look back and to look forward. What about the present moment? Is Jesus coming to our lives, to our communities, to our world today? Yes, Jesus comes to each of us in Holy Communion, in the smile of a child, in the kind word from an elderly woman, in the strength of a young man helping a person who is blind. Are we ready to receive Him whenever He comes? Perhaps Advent should help each of us to be more aware of those precious moments when Jesus comes to encounter us even in ways that we least expect Him. Who can help us to better prepare for Christmas and for each encounter with the living Christ?

When we think of the birth of a baby, we immediately focus our attention on its mother. During the Advent season there are two great Marian Feasts: December 8, the Immaculate Conception, and December 12, Our Lady of Guadalupe. Both of these feasts help us to focus on Jesus' mother. Both of these feasts honor Our Lady as she points out the way to prepare for the coming of Jesus. Her Immaculate Conception is a special gift from God to prepare her to be the first tabernacle where Jesus, the Word of God made flesh, dwelt for nine months. She, like John the Baptist, calls us to prepare ourselves by turning away from sin and being alert and ready to receive Jesus when He comes to us. We must remember also that, since 1846, under her title of Immaculate Conception, we honor Mary as the patroness of the United States. How can we help our country to, in the words of the Advent liturgies, "turn away from sin" and "prepare the way of the Lord?" Who can help us better to prepare for Christmas not only as individuals but as the collective people of God?

Today, December 12, we celebrate the feast of Our Lady of Guadalupe. Pope John Paul II proclaimed Mary, under this particular title, as the patroness of all America, since the beginning of Christianity in this hemisphere and her visit with St. Juan Diego. This celebration helps us to realize another "birth" of Jesus in the American continent. That is what Our Lady of Guadalupe concretely expressed by appearing as a pregnant woman. She left us her image wearing the black maternity band tied in the front. She also shows on her womb a small four-leaf flower with a circle in the middle which, for the indigenous people, symbolized new life, new birth. Who can help us better to prepare for Christmas, but the woman who is eagerly and reverently expecting the birth of her son?

We read in today's gospel for the Third Sunday of Advent (Matt. 11:2–11) that John the Baptist receives from Jesus the response that characterizes Him as the true Messiah: "the blind regain their sight, the lame walk, lepers are cleansed, the deaf hear, the dead are raised, and the poor have the good news proclaimed to them." These are the actions that Jesus invites all of us, His followers, to do for our brothers and sisters. Our Lady of Guadalupe, the first and best disciple of Jesus, gives us the example. She helped Bishop Juan de Zumárraga to see the truth; she asked St. Juan Diego to go to places that he "was not accustomed to visit"; she cured not only Juan Bernardino, Juan Diego's uncle, but many countless people who also considered themselves unworthy; she helped the indigenous people and the missionaries to "hear" her message; she gave hope to the indigenous people who felt doomed to extinction; above all, she proclaimed the good news to St. Juan Diego and to all the downtrodden. By her actions and words she calls us to solidarity with one another and particularly with those who are oppressed or marginalized.

Our Lady's request to the bishop and to all of us is: "I deeply desire a Temple to be built here where I can show my love, compassion, help, and protection to you, to all the peoples of this land and to all who will call on me with faith and trust." Throughout the years, we have taken literally the first part of her request and have built concrete "temples" (basilica, parishes, shrines) in her honor, yet we seem to have forgotten the second part of her request.

She does not want a temple solely so that we can go to honor her there together with her Son. She wants a temple to have a place where she can show her "love, compassion, help, and protection." How can she, how can Jesus, show love, compassion, help, and protection today if it is not through us? It is said that a statue of Christ was desecrated and the hands were broken. Then, someone placed a message that read: "I have no other hands but yours." How true is that saying particularly today when we Christians are challenged to be Christ for one another!

How can we give "help, compassion, protection, love" to those who are in need? The readings of today, the Third Sunday of Advent, seem to emphasize our responsibility in practicing the works of mercy and the social teachings of the Church if we are to follow Jesus' example as Mary did. The first reading that we heard today was taken from the prophet Isaiah (35:1–6, 10). It describes the joy and richness that is experienced when what is barren blooms and flowers with the splendor of God's presence, fostering acts of kindness and joy: strengthening "the hands that are feeble," making "firm the knees that are weak," and encouraging frightened hearts to "be strong, fear not!" This is the result of God's presence in and through each of us and once again all those who are in need will be healed: "Then will the eyes of the blind be opened, the ears of the deaf be cleared; then will the lame leap like a stag, then the tongue of the mute will sing."

Once again, if we look at this passage and examine how Our Lady of Guadalupe treated St. Juan Diego and the other persons mentioned in the apparition account we learn how to relate and to help one another:

1) Our Lady calls Juan Diego by name, "Juantzin, Juan Diegotzin," with the ending *–tzin* which means you are worthy of respect. *Juan Diego is a person*, not an object.

2) She gives him a message taking into account his way of thinking and using concrete expressions like "God, through Whom everything has life," and concrete symbols such as "music like birds singing," which drew the indigenous people to a sacred space. *He is understood* on his own terms. She incarnates God's word in a way he can understand.

3) She entrusts him with a message and a request, and sends him out on mission. In the process his self-esteem and self-confidence grow and deepen. *He is promoted* from a low-class "Indian" to a divine messenger.

4) She adopts his symbols in her own attire and appearance. In this way Juan Diego could understand the Christian message because these

indigenous symbols contain "seeds of the Word." Juan Diego did not have to stop being indigenous to become Christian. *He is accepted within his own reality.*

5) She accepts Juan Diego's apparent failure when the bishop did not believe her message, but she encourages her messenger to try again and again without being discouraged. She promises to be with him and to reward him. She calls him to be faithful, active, and committed. *He is challenged to mission yet supported in his deficiencies.*

6) She sends him not only to the bishop but to his own people in order to share with them the message of salvation as they build a temple, the living temple of God through justice and harmony among all peoples. *He is the first lay missionary on the American continent.*

7) She challenges Juan Diego to grow in faith, obedience, and the perseverance that will enable him to believe in himself as he carries out his mission. *He is liberated,* as he realizes his divine call.

When we are free to continue living the mission for which we were created, we recognize our greatest dignity as children of God together with all of our sisters and brothers. If we love Our Lady deeply, we need to imitate her as a follower of Christ. Like her, we must "raise the lowly" and liberate each other to recognize ourselves as the children of God ready to accomplish the mission entrusted to us, always remembering that Mary and God accompany us every step of the way.

Today's responsorial psalm reiterated God's action in and through us: "The Lord God keeps faith forever, secures justice for the oppressed, gives food to the hungry. The Lord sets captives free. The Lord gives sight to the blind; the Lord raises up those who were bowed down. The Lord loves the just; the Lord protects strangers" (Ps. 146:6–9). Likewise, Our Lady of Guadalupe was faithful to Juan Diego, ensured that Juan Diego and his people were treated with justice and dignity. She helped them to see the truth of Jesus as their Savior and raised them from the humiliation of the conquest. She showed tender love for Juan Diego and protected all his people.

Throughout Juan Diego's fulfillment of his mission to bring Our Lady's message to Bishop Zumárraga, there were many opportunities to practice patience, perseverance, and endurance. Even though Juan Diego had to wait long hours before he was allowed to speak to the bishop and had to go several times to deliver the message, Our Lady kept encouraging Juan Diego to be patient, to wait, to believe ("to keep his heart firm") despite difficulties, as the second reading of today encourages us to do during this time of Advent:

"Be patient . . . as the farmer waits for the precious fruit of the earth . . . you too must be patient" (James 5:7–8). In the end Juan Diego's mission was fulfilled beyond his expectations. This will also be the outcome for us at Christmas if we persevere and wait with hope and joy the coming of Jesus into our lives, into our communities, into our nation and world.

Who can help us better to prepare for Christmas? The Church in the season of Advent and Our Lady challenge all of us in a very gentle way to follow her example in carrying out the mission that Jesus has entrusted to us: to receive with love and compassion all those people that come to our parish and to our city seeking protection and healing for their sufferings. If we respond to them and to all our neighbors, we continue to build the temple that Mary requested *including the purpose* for which she wanted it: to offer *protection*, assuming the responsibility to defend together the rights of each person as rightful citizen of this earth; *help*, offering the gifts we have and receiving with gratitude the gifts others bring to create a more fruitful world; *compassion*, "suffering with" all those who are in need with a preferential option for the poor and humble; and *love*, living in solidarity with all peoples in their struggles, in their sufferings, in their joys, even if it requires the giving of one's own life for others.

Perhaps we, like Juan Diego, are somewhat fearful to accept this challenge. Yet we need to remember what we sang in today's Gospel acclamation: "The Spirit of the Lord is upon me, because he has anointed me to bring glad tidings to the poor" (Luke 4:18). We should remember also the words of Our Lady to Juan Diego when he felt scared and troubled: "Am I not here, your mother? Are you not under my shadow and my protection? Am I not your source of life? Are you not cuddled in my arms? Who else do you need?"

Who can help us better to prepare for Christmas? Definitely, Mary, His mother and our mother. So, filled with the hope that she brought to all of us at Tepeyac, we await a new coming of the Lord. May the flowers, the roses of "help, protection, compassion, and love" bloom and flourish "with joyful song" in our community, in our world. May Mary, Our Lady of Guadalupe, be with each of us as we go forward to share the good news of God's love that will manifest itself so fully in the babe of Bethlehem, the Incarnate Word.

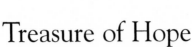

CHAPTER SEVEN

Treasure of Hope

Verónica Méndez, R.C.D.

I wish I could remember the year. I know it was during the 1980s—the supposed "decade of Hispanics." It was December and I was in Chicago for a meeting. We happened to be there the night the archdiocese was celebrating La Gran Posada that is held annually. We were hundreds, probably closer to thousands, and we went in procession to the Church of Our Lady of Guadalupe on the South Side of Chicago. But it was Tuesday night, the night for the novena to St. Jude. There were about seven little old ladies praying the novena in the upper church at the same time that we expected to be allowed in to conclude our procession and say our novena to Guadalupe. The priest instructed us to use the lower church because this time, every Tuesday, was for the novena to St. Jude. So we, hundreds of Latinos, processed down to the lower church not at all understanding why the seven or so little old ladies were not the ones being asked to use the lower church. Fr. Juan Huitrado was the homilist that night and I have never forgotten his words. He said to us in Spanish, "I think our Virgencita let this happen on purpose. We think we have arrived. There are hundreds of us here. We celebrate this posada every year. We believe, being the large number that we are, that we should have been given the preference of the upstairs church. But, no. In spite of our big numbers, despite of all the many years we have been 'en la lucha' (in the struggle), we have not yet arrived. Our Madrecita has allowed that we be pushed down to the lower church because she wants us to realize, we have not arrived. We still have a long way to go."

This time I do remember the year. It was 1531. La Conquista had happened and the original dwellers of this land had been thoroughly subjugated.

The Franciscans had been working long and hard among the indigenous tribes with not much to show for it. Of the few converts, one Juan Diego would be chosen to be the messenger of a dark-skinned Virgin, a Virgin that looked and spoke like him. The dialogue between Juan Diego and Guadalupe has always intrigued me. I am caught by this Virgin who had enough sense to come in a skin that was brown and a tongue that was Nahuatl. I marvel at her dress full of symbols familiar to Juan Diego's people and the black ribbon so clearly announcing her pregnancy. I am amused by the Amerindian to whom this vision is so real he asks her, "Did you sleep well?" But mostly, I am challenged. I am challenged by her request that we build her a house: "Deseo vivamente que se me erija aquí un templo . . ." I have never been able to listen to this dialogue between Mary and Juan Diego without feeling that Guadalupe is still asking that her home be built. That is, in reality, today, Our Lady of Guadalupe is still waiting for her temple.

Perhaps that is why she is such a perfect figure for Advent, our time of waiting. Advent tells us that Jesus, who was born so many years ago, is still waiting to be born in the hearts of us who have not yet conquered greed, discrimination, or the need to dominate. Our Lady of Guadalupe asks that a temple, home, be built where she can show her love for her children. A house, temple, was built and yet the home Guadalupe was asking for has not yet been built. Why is it that I hear Our Lady asking for her home? I have been in Hispanic ministry in this wonderful country of ours for almost the entirety of my forty-three years in religious life. We have gone through the wonderful years of the Encuentros. We have established the National Catholic Council for Hispanic Ministry and celebrated three national congresses of Hispanic Pastoral Ministry, *Raíces y Alas*. Our Latino theologians have organized themselves as the Academy of Catholic Hispanic Theologians of the United States (ACHTUS). The 2000 census states that there are 35 million Hispanics in the United States and recent updates of the census put the number now past 40 million, and those are the counted ones! The Latinos in the United States are presently some 40 percent of the U.S. Catholic Church. We have arrived, no? No!

Let me tell you stories and you will see why Guadalupe is still waiting for her home to be built. It was December of 1997 and one of the Mexican seminarians in Mundelein Seminary came to my office and, almost in tears, asked, "Sister, could you tell me why a pregnant woman is not a good symbol for Advent? And what is wrong with Americans that they don't like Mary?" As happens every seventh calendar year, in that year December 12 fell on the third Sunday of Advent. When I asked the student to give me the context of his question he explained that the director of liturgy in the parish where he helped out on the weekends was arguing that Guadalupe should not be celebrated that year because it fell on the third Sunday of Advent. The coinciding of these two feasts was a quandary for many parish directors of liturgy, especially if the parish had Mexicans. Liturgical directors felt caught. They *knew* it was liturgically correct to stay with Advent. But the more sensitive ones also knew there was no way Mexicans were not going to celebrate Guadalupe. I answered the student that there was no better symbol for Advent than a pregnant woman. After all, isn't Advent the season during which we wait, with our pregnant Mother, for the birth of her Son? I also tried to explain that Americans do love Mary. They just celebrate her differently than we Latinos. Guadalupe was celebrated in the parish that year with all the splendor the seminarian wanted, but at the cost of a lot more work for the Mexicans. The liturgical director insisted that anything that had to do with Guadalupe would not be allowed in the sanctuary except during the Spanish Mass because, said she, Guadalupe does not mean anything to English speakers. So all the scenery that had been erected the night before for the dramatization of the appearance of Guadalupe had to be taken down only to be put up again for the Spanish Mass and then taken down again before the last Mass in English.

"Deseo vivamente que se me erija aquí un templo . . ."

In some dioceses in our country Our Lady waits for her home to be built so that the Latinos may have a place in which to worship. I continue to be surprised when I find dioceses with a large number of Hispanics but no bilingual parish. Rather, perhaps there will be a few priests who run around saying Mass in Spanish in churches where *rent* is paid to the pastors for the use of the church. Obviously, they cannot get to all the corners of the diocese every week so many of these communities can have Mass in Spanish only once a month, if at all.

"Deseo vivamente que se me erija aquí un templo . . ."

In many other dioceses the cry of "you are building a parallel church" is still being heard. Here there is often awareness that a large number of the diocese is Latino. Often, there is a sincere desire to serve this part of God's people. Yet, here too, so often the lack of awareness of the imperialistic nature of U.S. culture gets in the way of service. In the effort of creating "one church" the Latinos must be served in the same way the English speaking are, in the same place and at the same time. This is considered treating them equally. There doesn't seem to be any awareness that this does not allow for a ministry that inculturates liturgy, customs, or spirituality. The desire to have "one church" ends up meaning the Latinos cannot be Latino in this church. The result so often, as we all know, is that the Hispanics vote with their feet and end up in one of the many evangelical churches who receive them with open arms and succeed so well in making them feel they are "en su casa" (at home).

"Deseo vivamente que se me erija aquí un templo . . ."

Of course, underneath my sense that Guadalupe is still waiting for her temple to be built is the suspicion that Guadalupe was not speaking of a brick-and-mortar temple at all. The indigenous peoples of these Americas had been contaminated with European diseases, killed by wars with the conquistadores, and later enslaved by them. She knew these natives were part of the human race her Son had died for. She wanted them treated as her children. *"No estoy yo aquí que soy tu madre?"* With the conquistadores had come Franciscans who sincerely wanted to share the Good News. These Franciscans were good enough missionaries to learn the language and customs of the native peoples and to patiently wait for conversions. But even those few natives who converted did not feel at home, "en su casa." Our Lady appears to let them know it is their home and she wants it built for them. But I hold that she was much more concerned with the people knowing, feeling, it was their home, than the structure of an actual physical building.

The year is 2005. Catholic immigrants continue to arrive on the shores, deserts, and mountain passes of the United States. The first place a Catholic Latino immigrant will usually go to is the church. He/she expects to be received. In too many places of our country this person is still often rejected. Either the staff does not speak Spanish or they may not like the color of the skin of the newly arrived. In some dioceses, incredibly, we are still hearing, "we do not have Hispanics here," or "our Latinos all speak English." When I hear this I have to wonder, who is cooking in their restaurants? Who is changing the beds in their hotels? Who is cleaning their offices?

Contrary to what many of us think, the history of the Catholic Church in the United States does not begin with the big immigration of the Irish, Germans, Poles, and Italians. The Church was already here in the Southwest and Florida long before these lands became a part of the United States. The first European language spoken in much of our territory was Spanish. Yet, in spite of this, it was 1970 before a Latino was consecrated bishop and in 2005, with 40 percent of the U.S. Church being Latino, only about 12 percent of the United States Conference of Catholic Bishops is Latino.

"Deseo vivamente que se me erija aquí un templo . . ."

In their pastoral letter of 1983 the United States bishops called Hispanics "a blessing." It is now 2005 and, sad to say, in far too many places Latinos are still treated as a problem, rather than a blessing for this U.S. Catholic Church. Our Lady waits for her temple to be built. It is a temple built with the stones of hospitality, warmth, and dignity. It is a temple that recognizes the "blessings" that come to it. It is a temple that widens to be inclusive of all peoples. It is a temple that stretches out to reach the lost and the ones who do not know the location of the temple. I also suspect that Guadalupe was not limiting her temple to the specific location of the hill of Tepeyac. She has been named Empress of the Americas and she looks for her temple in the entirety of this geographic area.

Advent is said to be a season of hope perhaps because without hope, one does not wait. I was told by a professor of homiletics that every homily must proclaim the Good News! I ask myself, where is the Good News in this homily? I find the Good News in Our Lady of Guadalupe herself, in this treasure of hope, in the fact that she continues to wait for her home to be built. Her waiting gives me hope that she sees better than I do, a future where her roses of compassion, acceptance, and inclusive harmony bloom even when they are not in season.

CHAPTER EIGHT

~

Juan Diego:
The Empowered Evangelizer

Anita de Luna, M.C.D.P.

The celebration of the feast of Our Lady of Guadalupe, *la Morenita*, is a celebration of the Mother of God, the feminine face of God, the miracle of Tepeyac, and perhaps most significantly—the genesis of Christian faith in the Mexican Americas. In contemplating the event of 1531 we remember Juan Diego the evangelizer, the mediator, the chosen one. Luke 4:18–19 reflects Juan Diego's invitation to collaborate in the Guadalupe mission. We read:

> The spirit of the Lord is upon me, because he has anointed me to preach the gospel to the poor; he has sent me to heal the brokenhearted, to proclaim liberty to the captives, and recovery of sight to the blind, to set at liberty those who are oppressed.

Juan Diego's response to the call of Guadalupe as the evangelizing chosen servant, the transforming humble one, teaches us a lesson on the virtues of the poor in our own calling to discipleship and evangelization.

Juan Diego, Nahua Culture, and Latino Cultures Today

God had given Juan Diego's people special gifts of dignity and beauty to share with humanity. According to Mexican scholar Miguel León-Portilla, the

Nahuatl culture was built on two basic metaphors: *Rostro y Corazón* (face and heart) and *Flor y Canto* (flower and song). These two metaphors focused on the formation of the person and on attentiveness to the beauty and dignity in his/her surroundings. God had favored Juan Diego's culture by creating a people of gentleness, humility, and awareness of God's creation. It is these gifts that prepared Juan Diego's heart and person to be a transforming evangelizer in the experience of Tepeyac.

Rostro shaped the exterior behaviors of the Nahua into harmonious, obedient, and accommodating personalities to serve the needs of others for the purpose of the community. *Corazón* spoke about the inner values of the indigenous that helped mold them into respectful, honest, and reliable individuals. Juan Diego illustrates these particulars of his personality when he tenderly directs himself to *la Morenita*, in his obvious concern for his uncle, Juan Bernardino, and in the respectful yet determined way he addresses Bishop Zumárraga.

In our Mexican American culture we see remnants of these virtuous behaviors in how soft-spoken many people are, in the honor paid to the elderly, in the pride parents take when children are mannerly, especially in greeting visitors and in politely excusing themselves. When we were children, how often did we hear our parents ask of us when visitors came, "ven a saludar" (come to greet), and how often have we asked our children "saluda mi hijita" (say hello, my child). When I grew to become an adult, after much study and academic degrees, my mother still asked: "¿Y con toda esta educación, aún sabes tratar a la gente?" (After all this education do you still know how to treat people right?) Education for my mother, as for many Latinas and Latinos, is about learning how to get along and respect others. I was the first in my family to earn a high school diploma and the subsequent degrees and my mother's question regarding education still resounds in my heart today. The value that we place on getting along with others, the appreciation for the child or adult who is "tranquilo" (peaceful), and the pride we take in having a harmonious home or parish community are all ways in which we keep alive and practice the virtues that the indigenous inculcated in their members.

Being a person of good heart and learning how to get along with others also included a reverence for creation and for the earth. There was a connection to the universe that put human life and our relationship to the power of the deities and of nature into perspective. Thus, we can understand Juan Diego saying of himself: "I am a wing, I am a tail, I am a leaf, I am nothing." His was a humility born of his very soul; he knew himself as a small creature in a universe that was overwhelmingly powerful and immense. In this understanding of humanity there was no room for a sense of superiority or self-pride. The intrinsic value of humility before the greatness of creation resulted in the formation of a cooperative individual who would be filled with integrity and truth about himself/herself and about others. To act contrary to what was interiorized in the culture was to sin and be at odds with the community.

In the account of Guadalupe Juan Diego is eager to be helpful to the *Virgencita* while also recognizing his own limitations. When he hears the *Morenita's* request that he go to the bishop on her behalf, he is quick to request that she send someone whose voice can carry her message effectively because he does not believe his voice has the influence her petition requires. In his heart of hearts Juan Diego recognizes that the appeal to the bishop will demand more than what he can offer, and he does not wish to be a hindrance to the Lady's mission. This indigenous sense of humility can sometimes become an obstacle for us who are of Latino heritage; for example in my ministry oftentimes I find myself asking parishioners to participate as lectors, catechists, ushers, or as other ministers and frequently the response is "hay Hermana, invite a otra persona porque yo no soy buena para eso" (Sister, invite someone else because I am not good for that). It takes much convincing to get the poor to feel comfortable with the leadership roles that are needed and that are rightfully theirs. There is an almost innate perception that others have more to offer than ourselves and can do things better than we can. Even after much education I find that among my Latina/o colleagues at the university we still hold back and either do not volunteer or do not accept invitations as readily as many of our non-Latino cohorts.

Through *Flor y Canto*, the fostering of an appreciation for beauty and song, the indigenous communicated with the divine through nature with its flowers, feathers, colors, stones, the songs of the birds, and the inspirations of poetry and music. This link of beauty to the holy is captured in one of the early catechisms, *Psalmodia Christiana*, written by the Franciscan friar, Bernardino de Sahagún. The missionary used metaphorical language to speak about spiritual thoughts, comparing the Our Father to a wristband of jade, ruby, and other precious stones and the prayers to the Blessed Mother to a necklace made of perfect flowers, glistening like precious jade, spreading their light. Beauty was clear and was appreciated in all that was pleasing to the eye, sweet to the senses, and delightful to the touch. The account of Guadalupe is replete with imagery: songs of the birds, the roses, the sun around the *Virgen*, the dew, and the quiet loveliness of the desert. The splendor that feeds the soul was a special gift from heaven to the people whose simplicity and humble place in the universe helped to prepare them for the Guadalupe message.

Appreciation of the beautiful continues to be a special cultural contribution of the indigenous people to society today. There is a delight in flowers, in gardens, the personal adornments in earrings, necklaces, and jewelry of all types. The personal enjoyment moves to the sacred in the color in liturgical rituals such as *posadas*, *matachines*, *pastorelas*, *quinceañeras*, all of which awaken the senses and stir the imagination.

Sitting with the poor I have frequently marveled at the importance placed on celebrations. For example, like many families my sister and brother-in-law often have barely enough to pay bills; yet when my niece turned fifteen years old they went for a bank loan in order to buy her a beautiful dress and provide her with a dance and a meal for three hundred guests. Never was there any discussion that the loan would be sought, not a second thought was given that there would be difficulty to make payments later. The importance of the *quince años* merited the celebration and it would be done. The festive beauty—colors, customs, food, and songs—that goes with memorable celebrations such as weddings, *quinceañeras*, *bautizos*, and first communions are non-negotiables for a people among whom beauty and fiesta run in their blood.

Juan Diego is very aware of the beauty that surrounds the Lady. He calls her *niña linda* (beautiful child), and the imagery of care and beauty continues to emerge in the many Guadalupe songs such as "Buenos Dias Paloma Blanca" (Good Morning, White Dove), "Desde el Cielo una Hermosa Mañana" (From Heaven, a Beautiful Morning), "A Tí Virgencita" (To You My Little Virgin), and many others. Consequently, the awareness of beauty and the presence of song were very noteworthy in the Nahua culture and we see a carryover into our celebrations of Guadalupe today with the use of color, *matachines* dancers, flowers, songs, food, and the many ways in which we enjoy and integrate beauty and tangible images in so many of our festivities.

The Call and Response

Juan Diego's God-given gifts were needed for the Guadalupana's mission. *La Virgen* recognized Juan Diego's goodness and dignity and confirmed her faith in him by entrusting him with a mission. Despite Juan Diego's reluctance to be her ambassador, the Virgencita knew that one of the best ways to evangelize Juan Diego as poor and rejected was to call him to evangelize others so that he would recognize his own gift. Juan Diego's participation in Guadalupe's mission makes it evident that we too are called to cooperate with a divine plan to transform society.

Juan Diego is the medium to bring about the transformation of an unjust society. Via Juan Diego, the Virgin brings about a new consciousness of the influence of the poor, who can and do evangelize the more fortunate. Juan Diego does not disappoint the Virgin, he succeeds in the mission entrusted to him, thus closing the gap between the voice of the rich and the poor. Juan Diego proclaims liberty to the captives and recovers sight for the blind because he speaks and persists until he is heard, revealing a new meaning and dignity for the oppressed. *La Virgen* not only makes Juan Diego equal to the Spanish leaders but also makes him the agent of his people's destiny.

The call to bring about change needed in society is issued for all of us catechists, theologians, teachers, parents, parishioners, and students. When I was in a small town as a director of religious education I was deeply touched by what transpired in the small parish over the period of time I served with the people. The day I arrived at the parish there were about twenty persons attending Mass on a Sunday. I met with some of the parishioners and asked why people had stopped going to church and what it would take to bring them back to share their faith in the church community. The people responded that there was discontent with the priest and many people were unhappy and thus were not willing to come celebrate at the church. The pastor had named himself president of the Guadalupana society and even held the keys to the parish hall exclusively so that parishioners had to climb through the windows of the building to carry on the activities of the parish. He had taken to scolding the people from the pulpit on Sundays and was denying communion to those persons with whom he had conflicts.

After some lengthy discussions the people decided to revive their faith community; I encouraged them and said I would help but they would need to lead. The mission was to transform the parish community and to regain their rightful role and power in their church. Several meetings with ecclesiastical leaders were held until the pastor was transferred. The parish community called upon their leaders and started a youth choir and an adult choir. They revived the Holy Name Society for the men and reorganized the Guadalupanas for the women. Catechetical programs became pivotal to the activities of the parish. One of the obvious problems was that the church building had been condemned and the parishioners had to celebrate in their neighbors' church rather than in their own. The people committed to raising the funds to build their own church.

The adults and children learned how to play instruments to form a choir, and little by little the choirs began to bring life and joy back into the celebrations at the church. Fundraisers at the market square also showcased the choir voices and the parish musicians' growing skill with their instruments. The choirs made uniforms and began to take great pride in who they were and what they did. Other parishes and surrounding towns began to invite the choirs to sing at their places and the parishioners' confidence grew as the church pews filled up again, people started smiling anew, and a festive spirit returned to their parish.

Meanwhile, the parish organizations grew and worked hard to raise funds to build their church building once again. It took two years to fill up the church, and it took eight to physically rebuild the church. The dedication of the new church was an event to remember; like Juan Diego the people felt empowered once they embarked on a mission to gain voice and came to a new recognition of their own gifts and power. Years later, that new church still sits in splendor filled to capacity, and the people of this small, seemingly insignificant town have a new consciousness of who they are and what gifts they have; they know themselves as capable of attaining their goals and transforming their surroundings. The young adults who are the parish leaders and catechists were once the participants in the children's choir whose songs brought back to worship an alienated parish community.

Like these contemporary lay leaders, it is Juan Diego who in his vulnerability carries out the *Morenita's* request and teaches us in the process that we must live in faith and that divine invitations come to us with an assurance of support, a promise that we never struggle alone nor in vain. We hear this same thought reiterated by the new evangelization that calls us to open ourselves up to be evangelized by the poor. Juan Diego was formed with genuine care for others and a consciousness of the presence of the divine in beauty and truth; thus he was ready to be the empowered evangelizer that transformed his society. What opportunities does our culture provide for us to contribute beauty and truth to our surroundings today?

Confronting Juan Diego's reluctance to be her messenger, the *Virgen* insisted that she had many others she could call upon but she was choosing him to be her evangelizer. Today each of us receives the same challenge as Juan Diego; it is only when we respond to being empowered that we transcend our personal insecurities and bring about transformation.

CHAPTER NINE

My Dear Juan Diego

Raymond Brodeur

My Dear Juan Diego:

Today, the universal Church remembers Our Lady of Guadalupe and you her trusted messenger. You, a poor Aztec peasant, endured the conquest and the domination of the Spaniards. Like millions and millions of women and men who live in our world, you seemed destined to disappear into the anonymous mass of people who count for nothing! Yet a momentous event transformed your life and, hundreds of years later, continues to inspire the lives of millions. All this started at the very dawn of day on Saturday, December 9, 1531.

As you were accustomed to doing, you walked around Mount Tepeyac on your way to receive the weekly teachings offered by the priests who had come to Mexico. Then you heard a very sweet and marvelous melody as you had never heard before. You took your time, stopped, and listened. When the song had ceased, beautiful words filled your ears: "Dignified Juan, dignified Juan Diego!" For a moment, you heard nothing but the pounding of your heart. You walked away from your usual route and climbed the hill from whence the voice was coming. At the summit of the hill, you encountered a beautiful Lady of resplendent brilliance.

It was important for her that you speak with her, that you tell her about your life as if you were speaking with your most trusted confidant. She wanted to listen to your voice and to learn your heart's intentions. Just like the Annunciation when she declared herself to be the servant of the Lord, you too presented yourself to her as an honest man anxious to accomplish the things divine that the priests, the representatives of the Lord, were teaching.

Dear Juan Diego, this first contact between the Lady from heaven and you seemed so simple and natural, yet it is incredible how it challenges us today. Your encounter situates us in the presence of two persons who mutually recognize each other as dignified children of God ready to accomplish his works. There is a quality of presence and a disposition toward one another which questions our very way of being present to others, our very postmodern materialistic ways of relating to each other and regulating the affairs of life. You and the Lady challenge us to ask what is our true dignity and real vocation in our modern world. You invite us to reflect on the nature of our life's vocation within the context of the various personal relations of everyday life. That is more important than all the world's projects of today and arises out of the very nature of being human!

Once the Lady recognized your dignity and situation as a son abandoned by others and even feeling abandoned by God, in the depths of your heart you became an accomplice of her project. The Virgin Mary, chosen to be the dignified human mother of the Creator of all persons and of all creatures, wanted to manifest and share with the poor and the dispossessed all her love, compassion, and protection. She herself, having recognized your suffering, your abandonment, and your innermost dignity, wanted you to make known her evangelical desires to the bishop of Mexico. Being the mother of God, she wanted the bishop to construct on Mount Tepeyac a home where she could welcome everyone who wanted to come with their miseries and pains and be consoled within the fold of her arms. Her proposal, reinforced by the promise that she would repay you and fill you with joy, produced an immediate and enthusiastic response, much like that of the first disciples whom Jesus invited to follow him: "Immediately, they left their nets and followed him" (Matt. 4:20).

The events that followed clearly show how many persons were blind to the truth because of their own preoccupations and obligations. Yet your generous acceptance and gracious willingness propelled you without hesitation to go to the bishop, the leader of this nascent church. But what happened?

You rushed without hesitation to the bishop's palace. Your audacity to insist on meeting with this very important person as a poor *indio* was repaid by a long wait. Once the meeting was finished, the attitude of the bishop let you know well in your heart that you were not believed. You felt deeply wounded. Your suffering was not so much due to the fact that you were not believed, but to the fact that you saw that the request of the noble Lady of Tepeyac would not be accomplished. The nonrealization of her desire was a thousand times more important than having been turned away. You would have known well, by your cultural experience of the times, that such an important man would hesitate to believe the word of a poor *campesino*. He had not yet learned to recognize in you the presence of God. Probably this was still unimaginable and impossible for him at this time.

After that, you went to the beautiful heavenly Lady and explained to her everything that had taken place and what she should do so as to be believed. Instead of choosing you, a poor Aztec, you who were nothing, it would be better to send an important person, someone who was credible, well known, respected, and esteemed. Such a person would be listened to and believed. In the logic of all human beings and especially of the colonial empire, you knew well that this was the only way to proceed.

However, this was not the logic of the heavenly Lady! She did not wish to send someone esteemed and respected by the conquering society. She wanted to send someone according to the choice and favor of God, someone filled with God's love and totally committed to God's will. She wanted as her messenger a person who would give his lively consent to her wishes ani-mated by faith and evangelical charity. As a good pedagogue of the ways of the God of Trinitarian love, she chose you, my dear Juan Diego, to lead the good bishop, who was certainly respected and anxious for the good establish-ment of the Church, to better discern and recognize this evangelical spirit. Her wisdom reflects the words St. Paul stated to the Corinthians: "For Christ did not send me to baptize, but to preach the gospel—not with the wisdom of human language, however, lest the cross of Christ be rendered void of its meaning" (1 Cor. 1:17).

Dear Juan Diego, please help us today to recognize the goodness and truth of this evangelical spirit that animated you, of that spirit that can truly liber-ate and enrich our humanity. Your second visit to the bishop places before our eyes the gestures and words of one who through fidelity accomplishes what has been demanded of him. In reality, no other reason or argument motivated you to return to the bishop's palace! The only reason you returned was the love and faith you had for the Lady whom you had recognized as the Mother of God. Even if the enthusiasm of the first visit had been replaced by uneasiness on this second visit, this in no way lessened your unquestioned conviction of her word and her calling.

Certainly you did not foresee that the bishop would once again listen to you and question you, replaying the scene of St. Thomas who after the resur-rection demanded tangible proof of the resurrection in order to believe (John 20:25). This was quite natural. This is the way human beings tend to react, particularly one with such a vast pastoral charge as the first bishop of Mexico.

However, your second testimony at least incited the bishop to listen closer, to ask you for something, whether or not he believed that your message was true. One will never know exactly what was on his mind, but we can certainly ask ourselves: what would have been our attitude in such circumstances? Would we not have responded in similar fashion?

Upon leaving the palace, you left with a problem which must have seemed impossible: how to prove the veracity of your mission with a sign when neither you nor the bishop had any idea what it could be. Your testimony alone had not been sufficient to convince the bishop. He must have a confirmation, some bit of irrefutable evidence! You had no choice but to report this to the Lady from heaven.

But, arriving at your home, you were immediately trapped by the realities of everyday life. Your elderly uncle was gravely ill and dying. He had need of help. In the very name of the charity taught to you by the missioners, you had to return rapidly to Mexico to search for a priest who could help your uncle in his dying moments. After that, you would have time to return to the affairs of the Lady from heaven. So, once again, the normal flow of things had to be interrupted.

Not wanting to be delayed by the urgency of your going for a priest, you decided to take a different route around Tepeyac. But to your great surprise and embarrassment, this beautiful child, the beautiful Lady, was waiting for you on this different route. She asked where you were going. Happy to see her and listening only to your heart, you asked how she was doing at the beginning of this new day: "My child, my most abandoned daughter, my Lady, I hope that you are happy. Did you awaken well at the beginning of this day? Do you feel well, my Lady and my child?"

Then you informed her that you did not want to trouble her heart, but you had to accomplish that which you knew to be your duty at this moment. You told her of your uncle, his illness, and your errand of mercy to bring him a priest. Then you promised to return and deliver her message, pleading with her: "My Matron, my Child, forgive me, have a little patience with me; I do not want to deceive you, my most abandoned Daughter, my Child. Tomorrow, I will come quickly."

In reality, there was another affair of God that pressured you at this moment, an affair, one could say, of the "domestic church." The good Lady made herself your ally. She informed you that she had already taken care of that which worried you and that your uncle had been healed. Then she told you that she had immediate need of you for another affair of God, an affair of the local and even universal Church. She remembered the discussion of your last interview with the bishop. In response to his request for a sign, she sent you to cut the beautiful flowers blossoming on the summit of Mount Tepeyac. She further instructed you to take these roses and deposit them at the feet of the bishop.

I can well imagine the surprise of the bishop, and probably your own, as you unfolded your *tilma*, the flowers fell to the ground, and you saw the image of the Lady from heaven engraved on your cloak! What an incredible confirmation! For you, it probably provoked the simple smile of complicity with the one whom you had never doubted. For the bishop, it must have been like a flash of lightning, a profound experience of faith that opened him to new aspects of the evangelizing project of God's love. Much more than a clear certitude arrived at through careful reflection, this lived experience with the word and the image of the Lady from heaven awakened him and his household to an even more beautiful taste of God's love. From this moment on, the building of her home, far from being a tiresome chore, was transformed even more radically into an evangelizing project of the Church in the service of the gospel.

Juan Diego, on this blessed day, we beg you to help us remain vigilant in appreciating our true human dignity as revealed by the Son of God. In our everyday life, we constantly act like the good bishop and devote our time to the affairs that seem important to us. We often place more emphasis on material accomplishments, on the completion of our projects, than on welcoming persons. If we constantly pay more attention to our own advancements and concerns rather than devoting time to those who live among us and have need of our presence, can we call ourselves children of God? Help us to listen to the beautiful sounds, to the beautiful music that calls us. Help us to hear those sounds that tell us: "My dear child, how are you behaving today? Where are you going in life? I have need of you to build up the Church desired by God who became flesh for us, the one engendered by the beautiful Lady from heaven."

Translated by Virgilio Elizondo

CHAPTER TEN

"Till There Was You"

Cecilia González-Andrieu

There were bells on a hill,
But I never heard them ringing.
No, I never heard them at all,
Till there was you.

There were birds in the sky,
But I never saw them winging.
No, I never saw them at all,
Till there was you.

Then there was music and wonderful roses,
They tell me, in sweet fragrant meadows of dawn and you.

There was love all around,
But I never heard it singing.
No, I never heard it at all,
Till there was you.

—from *The Music Man* by Meredith Wilson

It is doubtful that the composer of the Broadway musical *The Music Man* knew the story of Our Lady of Guadalupe, yet one cannot help but be struck by the amazing resemblance of what is described here to the events of Tepeyac. The story of Our Lady of Guadalupe and the song "Till There Was You" are both about the extraordinary power that Beauty has to completely change the way we experience the world around us. Until "there was you . . ."—our Lady up on the hill of Tepeyac—an entire people could not see, hear, or feel God's love. Today, she brings us that very same gift.

Can we hear the birds, or has the world grown silent for us? And most important, are we capable anymore of truly feeling ourselves loved by God?

During the extraordinarily new moments of the early Christian communi-ty's life the apostle Paul wrote to the Corinthians, "You are our letter, written on our hearts, known and read by all, shown to be a letter of Christ adminis-tered by us, written not in ink but by the Spirit of the living God, not on tablets of stone but on tablets that are hearts of flesh" (2 Cor. 3:2–3). There was a vibrant freshness and an amazing urgency to the word of God in the early church, and a sense that all of it was tied to our hearts, to hearts that were soft enough to both delight and bleed.

The loss of the aliveness of the world and of religious language is not something new to our generation, but rather has threatened every generation since religious discourse became habitual, and religious imagery ceased being astonishing. What is familiar, what is automatic, begins to disappear right before our eyes. And so language about God that communicates love and acceptance no longer reaches us. Back in the 1920s, scholars Viktor Boriso-vich Shklovsky and Benjamin Sher explained the silencing of the world this way:

> . . . held accountable for nothing, life fades into nothingness. Automatization eats away at things, at clothes, at furniture, at our wives, and at our fear of war. If the complex life of many people takes place entirely on the level of the unconscious, then it's as if this life had never been. And so, in order to return sensation to our limbs, in order to make us feel objects, to make a stone feel stony, we have been given the tool of art.

In order to "make a stone feel stony," in other words, precisely to return to the overly familiar the power of newness and surprise, we have been given art. These particular scholars do not say who this "giver" of art is, but as believers in a universe with an author, we recognize all gifts as coming from God. Thus, with this special God-given power art has to make creation visi-ble, relevant, and new, it is no coincidence that art and religion have been two sides of a coin for many millennia of human experience; "Till There Was You," although a patently secular love song, certainly can be sung as a song of praise to God. Thus, if religion does not also make a "stone feel stony," does not allow us to "feel" the love that is all around and wake us up to creation in its splendor and its sorrow, religion has become irrelevant and can scarcely announce the Reign of God. Art and religion must work together to help us see and hear that which has become commonplace, that which we can no longer glimpse or understand. Religion providing the content, art has the power to explode before our astonished senses. What is beautiful can make us look up and take notice of that which we need, vitally, to know.

The apparitions of Our Lady of Guadalupe fit into no stereotypes of Christian preaching that anyone could have conjured up in the middle of the sixteenth century; everything about this event was new, everything about the drama at Tepeyac spoke eloquently, not about a Reign of God yet to come in some other place, but about a Reign of God radically infusing our very world. Our Lady of Guadalupe came as a woman who knows that those around her need love, care, and healing. Because of her, all of us from Juan Diego to today can look up and feel loved.

Yet, from the vantage point of the twenty-first century, it is very difficult for us to see the newness in Our Lady of Guadalupe; her image has become overly familiar, reproduced on everything from tattoos to mugs and T-shirts. The miracle of her enduring presence on Juan Diego's *tilma* is locked away behind glass in a basilica, and many of us relate to it just as we would to any other nice painting in a museum which seems remote and, dare we say it? . . . pretty. Has Our Lady of Guadalupe become a stereotypical cliché which we no longer see? Not if we are able to see the intense beauty, the gift of artistic miracles which converge in this one event. Let's turn the clock back then and situate ourselves in the world that witnessed her irruption for the first time.

On the eve of the moment when the "Lady from heaven" called out to Juan Diego, his world, the world of the Aztecs and of the people of America, was going through its darkest hour. The contrast was savage, the tragedy unspeakable. The Aztec empire at the time extended from the Gulf of Mexico down into present-day Guatemala. Aztec culture was a hybrid of the civilizations they had conquered and supplanted—the Toltecs, Mayas, and Zapotecs. The indigenous Cuauhtlatoatzin, the future Juan Diego, was born into a society where religion and its aesthetic manifestation and expression held a privileged place in the community's life. Even as the conquerors were disembarking on the beach, the Aztec emperor and his court prepared to meet the Spaniards arrayed in their finest ornaments and carrying trays of the most fragrant flowers. Beauty and the constant terror of death existed side by side for the Aztecs.

The capital city of Tenochtitlan (Mexico City) was built on two islands in the middle of a lake festooned with floating gardens. Walls of purest white and causeways arrayed over canals connected the imperial city to the mainland. The effect was so splendid that the Spaniards dubbed it "another Venice." This was the world that Juan Diego and his community knew one day, and then it was no more. As one of the eyewitnesses describes it in a poem scholars date to the period,

> Nothing but flowers and songs of sorrow
> are left in Mexico and Tlatelolco,
> where once we saw warriors and wise men.
> . . . We are crushed to the ground;
> We lie in ruins.
> There is nothing but grief and suffering
> In Mexico and Tlatelolco,
> Where once we saw beauty and valor.

After Cortéz's victory, the native population, displaced and demoralized, was physically dying not only from the carnage of war but from European diseases. But, the natives were dying another kind of agonizing death . . . the loss of their identity and with it their will and desire to live. The anonymous poet of "Flowers and Songs of Sorrow" understood the place of beauty in the lives of the people, and in the end, he desperately clung to the image of flowers and sorrowful songs as the last vestige of their shared identity.

So we see here, not stony stones, but fragrant flowers carried by the nobles to greet Cortéz and flowers as the last breath of a dying people; it is flowers that Our Lady of Guadalupe offers as hope. As the conquered people understood all too well, without beauty the reasons to live disappear, without beauty what is good and what is true fades from sight. A stone that is no longer stony cannot be used to build anything. The tragedy of a people which had suffered cruelty at the hands of its own warrior class and now trembled in the grip of new warriors from distant lands, moved Heaven—and Beauty was sent.

Our Lady of Guadalupe came then (as now) as a dramatic narrative preserved in both poetry and a luminous painting. Everything about her encounter with humanity surprises. It is before dawn, and a poor widowed man, a native who has been baptized with a new name (which perhaps does not feel truly *his* yet), is on his way to church and to his daily cares. The first inkling Juan Diego has that something extraordinary is happening is the song of the birds. Not only is the song exceedingly beautiful, but it seems to him that the hills are answering. Juan Diego looks up from his lonely road, one that he has traveled many times over, he looks up surprised by encountering beauty in a world that had long ceased being beautiful. Juan Diego is seized by that beauty, grasped to a degree that turns into contemplation and leads him to ask difficult questions.

It is a singular moment of intense honesty; no fire and brimstone has been hurled at him, no eternal punishment has been threatened. None of the clichés of "conversion" are apparent here. Rather, Juan Diego is taken into his own heart, and into his own people's traditions to ask the questions that all of his people need to ask. The questions we today still need to ask, "Am I worthy of what I hear?" Without even glimpsing the Lady whose arrival the sweet music is heralding, Juan Diego, faced with the beauty of the world around him, has to come face to face with his own feelings of worthlessness.

A conquered people, a people who could no longer recognize their home, perhaps a people who also felt deep within them their own sin . . . were they worthy of beauty? It is their human dignity and that of their world that the beautiful music from birds and mountains comes to rebuild, and the process will not be easy. Juan Diego will be beset by doubt, by feeling himself a nobody, and by being treated as insignificant by the church authorities who are about to hear his astounding tale. The Lady, the young mother who waits just beyond the music, will ask him to believe, not only in the living God, in her Son who has redeemed the world; the Lady comes to ask him to believe in himself, in his own voice and to be a herald of his community's value and goodness.

Are we worthy of God's love? Is this question not the one that most often stands between us and God? Juan Diego even does a bit of rationalizing—this could all be a dream after all. He could be imagining all this. A person who has suffered much is afraid to believe in what is beautiful, because losing it again would be unbearable. Is this what Juan Diego is feeling? Will he and his people learn to believe? Have we learned to believe that we are worthy?

As Virgilio Elizondo has pointed out, the Guadalupe event "marked the birth of a new Church: the Word of God enriching the situation and bringing newness out of the old, beauty out of the chaos, family out of previous strangers and enemies." Yes, what Juan Diego and his community are called to by Our Lady is not a recovery of their old identity, broken and trampled by conquest, but rather growth, transformation, and the fostering of their own prophetic voice into a *new* humanity. The human cycle of conquered and conqueror, of master and slave, of powerful and insignificant will continue unless Juan Diego, and every single one of us, risks doing something different.

Mary, who dares to say that God throws the mighty from their thrones and lifts the lowly (Luke 1:51–53) is clear with Juan Diego that she understands the "lowly" cannot regain their voice alone. This is what her gift of beauty brings, for the cycle of oppression and oppressed to end, this new voice must arise from a place within the oppressed which is full of abundance, full of the expansive desire to share the world, not hoard it. Otherwise, although the positions will be reversed, the cycle will continue.

The conditions of mutual exclusion, suspicion, and exploitation which surround Juan Diego seem like one of the most basic tragic flaws of humanity. It is this world that lies just beyond the beauty of that hill where Juan Diego meets the Lady; it encircles him with its specter of poverty, of nonbeing, and of death. It is even made explicit in the narrative by his uncle's impending loss. Juan Diego veers off the road away from the Lady because his uncle is dying from the diseases brought by the Europeans. Juan Diego is frantic to find some help, some care for the dying man. This is important; we can see that the urgency of worldly cares threatens his journey toward regaining his voice just as surely as his self-doubt does. Yet, the cares are real, his uncle's death is real, the inability to find help for him is real. We want to walk toward a new being, but how can we, when the old being demands so much of us? The answer that Our Lady's story reveals is clear—God's Reign does not mean an end to worldly cares, nor does it demand that we ignore these in order to follow the path up the hill. No, God's Reign means we are not alone, that God takes those cares right into God. The Lady does not wait in the appointed place, but seeing Juan Diego's affliction comes down the path to meet him, and then assures him that his uncle will be well.

This is a moment in the story when the Christian must experience something like a mirror—on the one hand, we are Juan Diego, grieved, hurried, fearful, and yet, if the Juan Diegos of the world are to be helped to gain their voice, we must also be the Lady. We, like her, must be willing to go out of our way to walk toward those who need us. Like her, we must be willing to take up their cares with them, to lighten their loads, so they may continue to walk. Guadalupe's beauty is in her very dynamism, in her willingness to do what must be done, so that the voice of the new people of America will rise.

Beyond this, though, this moment in the story strikes us with the paradoxical nature of human existence. In the act of avoiding the Lady so he may get help for his uncle, we also witness a compassionate and desperate man, who, having already lost his wife, is now facing the death of another he loves. There is no shame for Juan Diego in carrying the burden of his loss. Rather, it is an emblem of those qualities in him which the Lady comes to re-awaken. In his smallness, and in his grief, Juan Diego stands as an instance of all those who, having very little, will give even that little away. Juan Diego represents an entire people, an entire world, and in the desperation of choosing between faithfulness to his uncle, pitted against the very real, and quite political, admonition from the Lady to confront those in power, we can recognize ourselves. This moment of conflict is pivotal to the story; as Aristotle pointed out many centuries ago, "pity is aroused by unmerited misfortune, fear by the misfortune of one like ourselves." We are moved by Juan Diego at this moment to look inside our own hearts. How many times have we failed at either of these options, the one of taking care of those who need us immediately in the here and now—as his uncle does—or the option of looking up, envisioning a different world, and defying the odds to raise our voices to build it? The intricate beauty of the Guadalupe story is that without shaming or blaming, it calls us to a better "us." The flowers are there, up on the hillside, incongruously growing in the icy ground, but we must go gather them.

As Pope John Paul II has reminded us, "true love sets no conditions; it does not calculate or complain, but simply loves." In the gift of exquisite beauty, of birdsong and flowers, of a woman who brings comfort and also challenges, and in a poor man who raises his voice and with it a people, we recognize this most difficult of callings—to simply love. And it is just at this moment that we look up, and the voice of God reaches us anew and renewed and enfolds us, like Juan Diego's warm mantle. The Lady brings the heavens in her starry veil, Juan Diego brings us and all the earth in his roughly woven mantle—and they both meet in the flowers, overflowing, in the miracle of the beautiful, incomprehensible, unexpected gift, of being simply loved by God.

CHAPTER ELEVEN

Converted by Beauty

Virgilio Elizondo

Just as the child in Elizabeth's womb leaped for joy upon hearing the greeting of Mary, so did Juan Diego and subsequently millions of persons throughout the ages who have encountered *Nuestra Señora del Tepeyac*. So it is truly proper that on her feast day we gather to praise and thank God for this marvelous gift to all the inhabitants of this land we call America. It is so precious because at a moment of devastating human pain, our loving God sent us this precious gift to soothe our pain and begin the healing. But the Guadalupe event would do much more than just heal: it would actually be the beginning—the birth—of something so beautiful that it had never before happened in the course of human history. It would be much more than the beginning of a new world; it would truly mark the beginning of a new humanity. The gift of Our Lady of Guadalupe to America is especially precious because God did not have to do this, yet God, out of the abundance of God's compassionate love and fascinating creativity, wanted to do this for us, for humanity. Through her, the pains and scandal of conquest would be transformed into the joy and glory of new life.

Yet it was not just a gift for the people of that time. It is a gift to all of us at every moment of our collective earthly pilgrimage, while equally a very personal gift to each one of us. A loving mother loves all her children, but the "all" does not replace the very special love and concern she has for each one in particular.

I am sure that if you were to ask any mother for her greatest wish it would be that all her children could gather together and get along well with one another. She would not want to make them all the same, but would rejoice

73

in the uniqueness of each one and their capacity to get along well with each other and help each other in any way possible. This was precisely the wish of our blessed mother when she appeared at Tepeyac in 1531. She wanted a temple—a home—where she could gather together all her children, all the inhabitants of this land. She did not ask for a home just for the native peoples, nor just for the Europeans or the Africans who were already arriving, nor even for the mixed-race *mestizo* children who were beginning to be born. She wanted a home—a temple—for all her children, all the inhabitants of these lands. A more radical and refreshing word could not have been proclaimed by anyone. No one would have dared or even wanted to make such a proclamation, for racial and ethnic divisions were the accepted and enforced order of the day. No one but the mother of infinite love made flesh could have dared to make such a proclamation.

The reality at this moment of history was that in these lands recently discovered by Europeans, people were being divided into all kinds of social classes: masters, craftsmen, servants, slaves, women, men, whites, brown natives, *mestizos*, *mulatos*, blacks, and many others. All kinds of classifications were being used to legitimize the segregation, subjugation, and exploitation of human beings. This went totally against the wishes of Our Lady who did not want to see her children trampled upon, humiliated, and abused. In her eyes and heart, every single one of the inhabitants was equally human, beautiful, and dignified.

Would the solution be to turn the natives against the Europeans? Would it be to return to a pre-European past? There was no return, of course, but whatever the injustices and pain of their indigenous past, the present appeared far worse. To the native peoples, it appeared to be hell on earth. In fact, hell could not have been worse. So, what was to be done?

In past times, the great gift of God's compassionate love in Jesus started when Mary of Nazareth said an unqualified "yes" to God's incomprehensible request that she become the mother of Jesus without having known man. She was asked to do the impossible. Through Mary's "yes," the almighty and omnipotent God took on flesh and was born as every other human being has been born! It was through Mary's "yes" that infinite love became human flesh with all the limitations, frailties, fears, and even temptations that are part of our human condition. And it was through this infinite love made flesh that God started the most marvelous adventure for the salvation of humanity.

Through the acceptance of Mary of Nazareth to be the mother of the redeemer, God had started the rehabilitation of our world, broken and dehumanized by centuries of sin. So too once again, at the beginning of this "new world" that had begun through the sinful greed and cruelty of men who would rob their victims of their fundamental dignity and worth, God sent God's own mother, Mary of Guadalupe, to begin the reconstruction of this horrible and chaotic mess. Sinful desires were behind the attempt of some to build empires of pomp, excess, and wealth through the exploitation of the poor and enslaved, but love wanted to build a family of goodness and compassion. This is no less than the forces of Satan versus the plan of God! The newly arrived conquerors wanted to build a kingdom of gold and extravagance while many of the newly arrived preachers of God wanted to build a kingdom of charity and concern. The former wanted to re-create the old world in these new spaces, while the latter wanted to truly build a new world freed of the excesses of the old.

Though the Christian missioners were heroically trying to build this new family of love, they appeared to be impotent against the forces of evil— weapons of war, whips, shackles, and even new diseases unintentionally brought in by the conquistadores. The missioners had a beautiful vision of building an evangelical kingdom upon earth, but the immorality and cruelty of the so-called Christians who had come to conquer and enrich themselves at any cost would be a constant obstacle to their best work and intentions. They prayed unceasingly for a breakthrough and their prayers were answered, but in a totally unsuspected way. Who would have believed that the chief missioner would be no one less than the very Mother of God and that she would bring this about with the cooperation of one of the conquered Aztecs.

Since the very beginning of the preaching of Jesus, the personal entrance into the reign of God, into the family of God's children, came about through the repentance and conversion that accompanied belief in the Good News. This entails a complete transformation in our ways of thinking and feeling, a transformation of both the mind and the heart. In the midst of the chaos brought about by sin, what does this repentance and conversion mean in 1531 and even today? What is the "Good News" that people are to believe in then and now?

The personal encounter with the celestial Lady on the summit of Mount Tepeyac and subsequently in the palace of the bishop brought about an incredible transformation within the minds and hearts of everyone. It dissolved the deepest and most impenetrable walls that kept people from entering as brothers and sisters into the household of God. Today, encounters with her continue to produce those same grace-filled effects.

For Juan Diego, his fellow conquered peoples, and any of us who feels inferior, unworthy, or undignified, Our Lady calls us to repent from the negative and dehumanizing images of ourselves. She calls us to believe in ourselves and accept that we too are created in God's own image. We must throw away the old self and put on the new one. Our Lady brings this about in a very human way: she engaged Juan Diego in intimate conversation and confided an important mission to him. She, the celestial Mother of God, treated him like an equal. She treated him like a human being! In her presence, he is fully a human being! In her presence all the derogatory categories he has been subjected to dissolve and he experiences himself for what he truly is: a dignified and noble human being! This indeed is Good News. We are not what the sinful world says that we are. Through the encounter with Our Lady, we recognize ourselves for what we truly are: beloved children of God.

For the native world, culture and tradition were passed on to the next generation by the maternal uncle. The dying Juan Bernardino symbolized the absolute end of the native traditions and culture. It seemed that their cherished ways of life would be gone forever. But as so often happens, God had other plans. In the healing of Juan Bernardino we see the restoration of the traditions and culture of the ancestors. They were not false or diabolical, nor were they opposed to the Christian faith. Their ways would indeed be converted to Christianity, many of their ways would be modified and even enriched, but not at the cost of abandoning the sacred ways of their ancestors. They would come into the Christian family not deposed of their cultural treasures, but rather enriched with the incarnation of Christianity in these lands. They in turn would enrich the universal Christian family with all the treasures of their spiritual heritage. Today, this is the uniqueness, beauty, and wealth of our *mestizo* Christianity—a rich blend of the medieval Christianity of Europe with the deeply religious traditions of native America.

This healing of Juan Bernardino—custodian and transmitter of tradition—is important for us today. Often, in the face of the dominant culture and the latest fashions and styles, we might begin to think that the traditions and customs of our parents and grandparents are backward, antiquated, and embarrassing. Yet our traditions are sacred. They are not perfect and beyond improvement, for no culture is without its expressions of sin. But they are sacred, beautiful, and life-giving for they connect us with our roots, with the very roots of our earthly existence. So, just as Our Lady healed Juan Bernardino and thus guaranteed the continuation of the native customs and traditions, she reinforces and brings new energy into our customs and traditions, which are constantly challenged and threatened by globalization and the dominant material cultures of today. Fidelity to Our Lady guarantees the survival of the ways of our ancestors creatively integrated with the advances of the modern world. This is certainly Good News, for we will neither disappear as a people nor be isolated from the rest of humanity. Rather, in the give and take with other peoples, we will continuously contribute to the growth and development of the new humanity—the temple of Our Lady wherein no one will ever be excluded. This indeed is joyful Good News.

Conversion to the Good News of Jesus is never final and absolute until we see our God face to face at the end of our earthly life. So the bishop, the one designated as the primary evangelizer of the new world, also had to be converted. If Juan Diego had to convert from not believing in himself to seeing himself as a full and dignified human being, Bishop Juan de Zumárraga, the Europeans who considered themselves superior to the natives, and all people who consider themselves superior to others are called to repent from the sin of arrogance. They are called to no longer think of themselves as more important, nobler, more dignified, more worthy, and therefore authorized to insult, ridicule, and subjugate others. Repent and convert! Here the "Good News" might at first appear as "bad news" for it will mean thinking less of ourselves. Yet it is in this letting go, in our willingness to think of ourselves as less than society makes us think of ourselves, that we will gain a new freedom to be truly ourselves. It will be difficult, yet most liberating and life-giving for only in letting go of the categories of superior and inferior, dignified and undignified, worthy and unworthy, noble and commoner can we all confront the Juan de Zumárraga tendencies that lurk inside of us and enter into the joyful freedom of the children of God.

Our Lady, not through threats or condemnations, but through inspiring music, intimate conversations, and a beautiful self-portrait brings about the repentance, conversion, and belief that allows everyone to let go of their limiting and destructive self-images and see and appreciate themselves as God sees and appreciates all. The abiding presence of Our Lady invites each and every one of us into her family. She urges us to celebrate her feast in her home where we gather without any dehumanizing distinctions to celebrate the Eucharist in which her beloved son, Jesus Christ, continues to offer himself to us as the bread of eternal life and the one true source for the unity of humanity. She came to prepare the home where we could come and meet her son who was and is the first-born of the new creation: a humanity of radical equality and harmonizing unity. The repentance, conversion, and joyful belief we experience in the encounter with *Nuestra Madrecita de Guadalupe del Tepeyac* prepare us to receive her son into our lives in the table fellowship of her home.

In encountering Our Lady of Guadalupe today, we, like Juan Diego before us and all the peoples of previous generations, experience the joyful conversion to new life, to the life of the new humanity. Like Juan Diego, today we are invited to experience the beauty and delicacy of Our Lady's inviting presence so that we too will leap for joy, a joy that only God and God's mother are capable of producing in us.

Santa María de Guadalupe, come to us as you came to Juan Diego so that we might believe in ourselves as you believe in us. Come to us as you came to Juan Bernardino so that we might value, celebrate, and transmit the sacred traditions of our parents and grandparents. Come to us as you came to Bishop Juan de Zumárraga so that we might listen to the poor and simple of society and hear the call of God through their cries for recognition, understanding, and appreciation. Let us all work together to build that temple you requested: a space of universal welcome and fellowship for all the peoples of this hemisphere. Whether it is in our homes, our neighborhoods, our cities, our nations, or the world, let us do all we can to break down the walls of prejudice and build up the temple of the new humanity, a living temple of love and compassion. Let our untiring efforts become the beautiful and alluring melodies that will attract all peoples to your holy mountain and through you to the great banquet table of our Lord Jesus Christ.

CHAPTER TWELVE

~

The Virgin of the Massacre

Jeanette Rodriguez

The parish I attend has a sister parish in Chiapas, Mexico, where the Mayan parishioners have a great devotion to Our Lady of Guadalupe. Yet, as of 1997, they do not usually refer to her as the Virgin of Guadalupe, but as the Virgin of the Massacre. In 1997 some 250 people fled their villages and took refuge in a town called Acteal. In the hermitage there they knelt and prayed for peace. Most of the devotees were refugees—primarily women and children—from the violence that frequently has plagued their region. At that time para-militaries terrorized the people and on this particular day, December 22, 1997, the paramilitaries entered the chapel and riddled its adobe walls with bullets. Many people escaped into the hills; a large group threw themselves into the ravine. Witnesses say the massacre took about seven hours and forty-six people were killed. In that dark moment of bullets riddling their place of prayer, the paramilitaries also took the community's beloved Virgin of Guadalupe and broke it into pieces. On that terrible day, the people of Acteal mourned the Virgin of Guadalupe, whom they said had died along with their sisters and brothers.

But a few years later survivors of the Acteal massacre carried a little statue of Guadalupe on their shoulders up the hill, daring to reenter the place of the 1997 massacre. The Virgin's visit on Palm Sunday was as much a celebration as a triumph. Although the place where this destruction and murder occurred was almost deserted, those who had returned greeted the pilgrims and celebrated the arrival of *La Virgen* in much the same way every community does around the world: with music, flowers, and, in this particular cultural medium, fireworks and palm leaves. Four indigenous women carried

Guadalupe, who was dressed in the typical clothing of local indigenous women, her head covered with a black veil. She sat as the fragrance and smoke of the flickering candles created an aura about her. The survivors of the Acteal massacre wanted to bring the Virgin of Guadalupe to this particular village, past the military barracks, and into the place that was once the center of the paramilitaries. They wanted the Virgin of the Massacre to accompany them on their journey of healing and reconciliation, just as she had accompanied them during the massacre, just as she had accompanied their indigenous ancestors after the conquest nearly five centuries ago, just as she continues to make her presence known in an intimate, consoling way to every devotee who calls out her name.

One local leader explained it this way: "After the massacre we put her back together with a bandage. That was how she was resurrected. The Virgin saw everything on that day and now she is complete. This is why we gave her a new name—the Virgin of the Massacre. The displaced and the communities recognize the presence of God in the Virgin of the Massacre. We feel her presence in the village. She unites us with regard to differences; she unites us because she is the mother of everyone; she intercedes on our behalf with God. We feel her presence in our suffering, in our dreams, and in our hope."

For these faithful in Chiapas and many indigenous, Latinas, and Latinos in the Americas, and in particular Mexico, the feast of Our Lady of Guadalupe, while mediated through a particular culture (in this case the Mexican and Mexican-American culture) tells a universal story that makes God's presence known in the world. Contextually it is a story about betrayal and trust, destruction and hope, death and resurrection. In many ways it contains the Paschal mystery of the Mexican people and their resurrection into a new creation through the mediation of Guadalupe.

The human condition is such that we need to hear the promise of peace for our hearts, even (and especially) in the midst of our most desolate and darkest moments. We need to be reassured that we are not alone in the world and that there is a loving God who continually seeks us out and chooses to live among us, if only we have the eyes to see and the ears to hear. Our sight and hearing of the deeper realities in our lives are also necessary when we cross cultural boundaries and attempt to understand the diverse ways in which God chooses to reveal God's self. It is this desire to be open to finding God in all things that leads Guadalupe's faithful—including us today—to the narrative, image, and devotion to Our Lady of Guadalupe.

The year is 1531, ten years after the Spanish conquest of the indigenous people in central Mexico. Like our own Abraham and Sarah, the Aztecs were a deeply religious people who had left their land in response to divine instruction so they might be led to a land flowing with milk and honey. The sign they were to look for was an eagle perched on a cactus with a serpent in its mouth. This "sign" sat on seven lakes and upon those lakes the Aztecs centered their empire, one of the greatest civilizations in Mesoamerica. Like all empires, the Aztecs built theirs on conquest and consolidation of existing people. The Spanish, similarly, replaced the Aztecs through the brutality and violence of the conquest, a dynamic of oppression felt down to the present day in events like the Acteal massacre and other atrocities committed against indigenous peoples.

The protagonist of the Guadalupe story is a Christian neophyte named Juan Diego. On Saturday morning, December 9, 1531, Juan Diego is on his way to Mass and catechetical instruction. As he makes his way, he passes over the hill of Tepeyac, the ancient site of the great earth goddess Tonantzin (which in Nahuatl means "our mother"). Suddenly Juan Diego hears beautiful music. Following this music, he encounters a woman who speaks to him not in the language of the conquistadores, but rather in the language of his people, Nahuatl. She says to him "Juan Diego, the smallest of my children, where are you going?" It must have been something about her that he recognized, because the story says that he falls on his knees and says to her, "I am going to *your* house, in order to hear of the divine things our priests tell us." Tonantzin-Guadalupe responds, "Know and understand, you the smallest of my children, for I am the holy Virgin Mary, mother of the true God, *por quien se vive*, for whom one lives. I have a great desire that there be built here a temple so that I may show forth my love, my compassion, my help, and my defense, to you, to all of you, to all the inhabitants of this land, to all who call upon me, trust me, and love me. I will heal your pains, your sorrows, and your lamentations, and I will respond."

It is here—in the recognition of one for another—that the possibility for intimacy and joy is experienced through the grace of consoling presence. This is not unlike our readings today from Zechariah and Luke, where the indwelling of God and God's presence bring consolation and allow for a genuine intimacy that ultimately lead to the joy and peace that only our God can offer us. This compassionate presence is possible even in the midst of great strife and grief and pain. You would think that this kind of destruction is a story that only can make reference to what happened in past situations like the age of Spanish conquest, but tragically we know that we live in a deeply conflicted world where many people and families and communities are suffering.

Our Lady of Guadalupe appeared to Juan Diego; Our Lady of Guadalupe witnesses the suffering of all who are brutalized; she is present to all who call upon her, love her, and trust her. She hears our lamentations, our pains, our sufferings, and she responds with the love and tenderness of an ever-present mother. She responds in manifesting the love and compassion of a God who fulfills God's promises, and she offers help and defense in a variety of creative ways. What I find fascinating is that with experiences of grace like a Guadalupan encounter there is always an *intercambio*, an exchange or reciprocity that takes place, whether it's between her and Juan Diego, or the exchange of the flowers and the intimate words, or with the devotee with the exchange of prayers and flowers, thanksgiving, and renewal. In the case of the Mayans, I have heard testimony of their horror and accompanied them in the midst of that brokenness, but also witnessed how their faith enabled them to put her back together and in so doing put themselves back together because of their devotion to her. Guadalupe has touched the hearts of many who have suffered because of violence, war, poverty, marginalization, and isolation. She is also present to us as we struggle through our fears and despair. She urges us and the smallest of her children to guard in our hearts the certainty of her love and compassion for us.

Today we celebrate the feast of our Lady of Guadalupe, one more opportunity to rejoice in the faithfulness of a God who longs to be in our midst. The prophet in today's readings, Zechariah, rejoices in that knowledge, rejoices in the fact that this God who has chosen us desires to dwell in our midst. As Zechariah states, God promises "I will come and dwell in your midst" (2:14) and be personally present to us. One of our responses to that desire, that love, that presence, as we heard in our reading from Luke, is recognition. Zechariah recognizes the presence of God among us people. The child within Elizabeth recognizes Mary and whom she carries and for this reason, leaps in Elizabeth's womb (Luke 1:41–44). For those who recognize the Lord in our midst, the fundamental and spontaneous response is joy.

In the Christian liturgical calendar, the four weeks of Advent which precede Christmas are a time of waiting and anticipation. Advent is a time when we recall the prophets of the Hebrew scriptures, who continually ask us and remind us to believe the promises of God, to believe in the desire of God to dwell with God's people. And so we raise our voices and pray to this God who not only proclaims these promises, but also fulfills them. We unite in this Eucharist not only with our ancestors whose faith is remembered in the Hebrew and Christian scriptures, but with our ancestors of the Americas and all our places of origin, as well as the sisters and brothers with whom we share this hemisphere and this world today. In many ways God fulfills the promises of old; in many ways God makes God's love manifest and ultimately God chooses those people that the world rejects in order to make God's power, God's love and mercy, revealed in a transformative way.

Only through God can we attain a hope and peace that dispels the darkness that we experience. Our God is a God who sends us signs. Our God is a pregnant God: pregnant with hope, pregnant with possibilities and the fullness of being human. Ultimately this God is a God of life "por quien se vive," a God of life for whom one lives. May the sign of Guadalupe's love and concern for all of us fill us with consolation and peace, with the sustained recognition of God's love, and with the joy to celebrate that love with each other. May this Advent season give us the wisdom to continue our wait, our joy, continue our remembrance of Christ once born and our anticipation of Christ coming again. For our God is a God who sends us signs which point us to the land and place of hope.

CHAPTER THIRTEEN

~

Why Would Lutherans Celebrate the Virgin Mary of Guadalupe? A Theological Meditation

Maxwell E. Johnson

Today, December 12, is not only the Third Sunday in Advent on our liturgical calendar. For several Christian people throughout the world, especially
Mexican and Mexican-American Christians, today, as you may know, is also
the celebration of the Virgin Mary of Guadalupe. It is the commemoration of
her sixteenth-century December 9–12 appearances to Juan Diego, the recent
Nahuatl-Aztec convert to Christianity, whose *tilma* or cloak bore and continues to bear what so many still claim is the miraculous imprint of her image,
the image of the Brown Virgin (*La Morenita*). She is an indigenous *mestiza*
clothed with the sun and wearing the *cinta*, the band of pregnancy, standing
on the moon, head bowed and hands folded in prayer, and borne aloft by an
angel of the Lord.

Even so, however, since this event and image are so obviously Roman
Catholic and clearly part of the self-understanding of Mexican and Mexican-
American Roman Catholics, why would we Lutherans, even Hispanic/Latino
Lutherans, want to celebrate or pay attention to Mary of Guadalupe? What
can she possibly say to us in this time of mid-Advent as we draw so close
again to the Nativity of our Lord, to the annual celebration of Christ's birth?
And is it not Christ's Incarnation and birth we should be talking about and
preparing for and not wasting our time today on some superfluous and
perhaps even questionable Mexican Catholic devotion to and pictorial

representation of the Virgin Mary? I suspect many Protestants, even some of our fellow Lutherans, would strongly feel that way.

And yet I wonder. As we become intentionally a more multicultural church in the United States, as we seek to be open to the experiences and gifts of the other at our doors and at our borders, and as Hispanic/Latino people come in increasing numbers to Lutheran and other churches, is it not necessary for us to listen to their stories and to embrace their images and symbols? It is often said, with some exaggeration, of course, that "not all Mexicans are Roman Catholics but all are *Guadalupanos*." Hence, the story and image of Guadalupe might well seek and find a place in our own lives and Christian identities as "Lutheran Christians," even for us Anglos. Note, please, I did not say that we Lutherans should "use" Mary of Guadalupe in order to attract Roman Catholic Hispanic/Latinos to our churches or try to make "Lutheran converts" out of Hispanic/Latino Catholics. Such deceptive use of the cherished religious symbols of others has no place among us! But Mary of Guadalupe may well find her own home among us as she comes along with others into our midst and into our congregations. In fact, there are signs throughout our country that she is already here, with one of our newest parishes in Irving, Texas, bearing the name *La Iglesia Luterana Santa María de Guadalupe*.

Ever since I spent time in Mexico and visited her basilica in Mexico City over thirty years ago, images of Mary of Guadalupe have been a presence in my life. During Advent in the days prior to December 12, in fact, my family and I often hang a tapestry of her facing out on the inside of our front door, which is then illumined by the lights inside our house. Just two years ago on December 12, having ordered a pizza from Bruno's Pizza, *the* place for pizza in South Bend, Indiana, a young man who was Hispanic/Latino came to deliver it. Pointing to the tapestry, he said to me, "It is beautiful." And, in response, I said something like, "Oh yes, today is her feast. Happy feast!" And he said, simply, "She's my Mom." Not in a formal sense of "She's my *Mother*," but with the simple and beautiful language of intimacy and rela-tionship, "She's my *Mom*." Now, I don't know if this person was Roman Catholic, had any real religious background whatsoever, or was a member of one of the numerous fundamentalist groups, which seem to be attracting large numbers of young Hispanic/Latinos. But I began to ask myself from that moment on, "If this person were to come into a Lutheran congregation would we tell him that *he* is welcome but his 'Mom' is not, even though his 'Mom' is also the Mother of Jesus, our brother, in her Mexican appearance?" I think not! I believe, however, that there are other reasons beyond hospitality, openness to the other, and cultural sensitivity that might provide reasons as to why we, as Lutherans, as Hispanic/Latino Lutherans and others, might want to celebrate the Virgin Mary of Guadalupe.

We Can Celebrate Mary of Guadalupe Because She Proclaims to Us the Gospel

First, I believe that we Lutherans can celebrate Mary of Guadalupe because, like Mary herself in her great New Testament hymn of God's praise, the Magnificat, she proclaims to us the gospel, the Good News of our salvation in Christ, the Good News of God who scatters the proud, exalts the lowly, fills the hungry with good things, and remembers his promises to Abraham and his children forever.

The great New Testament scholar, the late Raymond Brown, once wrote that Our Lady of Guadalupe "gave the hope of the Gospel to a whole people who had no other reason to see good news in what came from Spain. In their lives the devotion to Our Lady constituted an authentic development of the Gospel of discipleship." Rev. Bonnie Jenson, former executive director of the Women of the Evangelical Lutheran Church in America, has also drawn attention to Mary of Guadalupe:

> I was deeply moved by the story of the poor man's vision of the Lady of Guadalupe. I was struck by how lowly, insignificant people have to beg the church to regard them with the esteem with which God regards them. We are not sure whether Mary appeared in a vision to this poor man. Perhaps we have our Protestant doubts. Yet even if we question the vision, the tragic truth remains: the poor and lowly often have to beg the church to proclaim and live out its message of a merciful, compassionate God!

We can celebrate the Virgin Mary of Guadalupe, then, because she proclaims to us the Gospel and because the message of Mary of Guadalupe is the same as that of Mary's own Magnificat of praise in the Gospel of Luke. Indeed, in so many ways, Mary of Guadalupe is simply the Mary of the Bible.

We Can Celebrate Mary of Guadalupe Because She Embodies for Us God's Unmerited Grace

A second reason why we might celebrate Mary of Guadalupe as Lutherans is that she embodies for us in a special way God's gracious act of salvation,

God's own unmerited and free grace. How quickly we Lutherans seem to have forgotten Martin Luther's own high regard, esteem, and praise for the Blessed Virgin Mary in his life and writings, even long after the Reformation had begun. Contemporary Luther scholar Eric Gritsch summarizes Luther's views, noting that for him "Mary is the 'Mother of God' who experienced his unmerited grace. Her personal experience of this grace is an example for all humankind that the mighty God cares for the lowly just as he cares for the exalted."

It is precisely the language of God's free grace that several contemporary Catholic authors use to speak about Mary of Guadalupe today. That is, according to them, the God proclaimed in the Guadalupan story is none other than the God-who-is-for-us, characterized by a consoling, nurturing, loving, forgiving, maternal presence and an unconditional love that is a grace-filled gift to humanity. And, if so, then the story of Mary of Guadalupe is precisely a proclamation of the God who justifies "by grace alone." And that this gift is received "through faith" is surely exemplified in the response of Juan Diego, who, like Abraham and countless prophets in the Hebrew Bible before him, interprets this encounter as a call to his own prophetic ministry both to his own people and to the governing (ecclesiastical) author-ities to whom he was sent. It must be recalled here that in contrast to several other visions of Mary throughout history, especially the more modern ones, Mary of Guadalupe asks for *nothing* to be done other than the building of what she calls a "temple." And this temple is itself to be nothing other than a place or "home" where all peoples might encounter divine love, compas-sion, help, and protection, and where their laments would be heard and all their miseries, misfortunes, and sorrows would find remedy and cure. In other words, this "temple," this "Beth-El" (House of God) of the Americas was (and is) to be a place where the God of unconditional love, mercy, compas-sion, grace, and forgiveness is proclaimed and encountered.

Even the implications and call for justice and liberation so often associ-ated with Mary of Guadalupe are also consistent with our understanding of justification by grace through faith. From within his Reformed theological perspective Daniel Migliore writes of the relationship between the sover-eignty of grace and the pursuit of justice exemplified in Mary's Magnificat: "Neither the biblical portrayal of Mary's passion for justice expressed in the Magnificat nor the classical Reformed emphasis on the sovereignty of grace lead to passivity or complacency. On the contrary, acknowledgment of salva-tion by grace alone goes hand in hand with a passionate cry for justice and a transformed world." If Migliore himself is not concerned specifically with

Mary of Guadalupe in this context, the parallels are obvious. As in the Magnificat so in Guadalupe is manifested Mary's zeal for God's honor, which, perhaps today more than ever, has led to a spirit of resistance against racial, social, and economic injustice in the world. At times, that rebellion and resistance may indeed be transferred more to revolutionary ideologies than to the biblical God of justice and/or righteousness. But the persistent presence of the Guadalupan image often associated with movements of rebellion and resistance nonetheless keeps open the possibility of hearing God's concern for the poor and its implications expressed so powerfully in Mary's own biblical proclamation, her Magnificat. To be justified by grace alone sets one free in the name of God to risk oneself and one's identity in the pursuit of God's own justice and righteousness for the world.

I would like to suggest that we might best appropriate the story and image of Mary of Guadalupe under the category of "parable," that is, "Mary of Guadalupe as Parable of Justification," or, "Mary of Guadalupe as Parable of the Reign of God." By the use of the word "parable," I mean how the Guadalupan story actually functions. Contemporary New Testament scholarship on the parables of Jesus has come to emphasize, in the words of Nathan Mitchell, that parables function as "stories that defy religious conventions, overturn tradition, and subvert the hearer's expectations" about how God is *supposed* to act in the world and, in so doing, "make room" for the inbreaking of God's reign. If contemporary biblical scholarship is correct, the parables of Jesus, as "reversals" which make room for the "advent" of the reign of God as surprising gift and invite the "action" of response to that reign, point unmistakenly to Jesus as the Great Parable of God Himself. Indeed, it is precisely the Crucified One who functions as the ultimate parable of divine reversal and salvation, especially as this is proclaimed by St. Paul in 1 Corinthians 1:27–31:

> God chose what is foolish in the world to shame the wise; God chose what is weak in the world to shame the strong; God chose what is low and despised in the world, things that are not, to reduce to nothing things that are, so that no one might boast in the presence of God. He is the source of your life in Christ Jesus, who became for us wisdom from God, and righteousness and sanctification and redemption, in order that, as it is written, "Let the one who boasts, boast in the Lord."

The narrative and the widespread presence of the image of Mary of Guadalupe can certainly be interpreted then as functioning parabolically in the same sense as the biblical parables themselves. For the Guadalupan story is precisely a parable of the great "reversals" of God, the subversion of both indigenous and Spanish cultural-religious worldviews and assumptions, standing them on their heads, in order to "make room" for something new. Juan Diego is none other than precisely one of the "low and despised in the world," who, in this encounter, becomes himself the prophet or messenger of the reign of God even to the ecclesiastical authorities. As an indigenous *layperson*, he subverts even the heavily clerical leadership structure of Spanish colonial church life. It is no wonder that, increasingly, Juan Diego is becoming today the model for the ministry of the laity, the concrete example of the priestly ministry of the baptized—the "priesthood of all believers" in our traditional terminology—within especially Mexican and Mexican-American contexts. Nor is it any wonder why early ecclesiastical responses to the Guadalupe event would have been so strongly negative. Then, as now, Guadalupe challenges the wise, the powerful, the noble, and the strong to a new conversion to the presence of the reign of God as located precisely in the weak, the lowly, the despised, and the rejected. This is nothing other than what we Lutherans like to call a *theologia crucis*, a "theology of the cross." For, like the parables of Jesus, Mary of Guadalupe, as "parable of the reign of God," or "parable of justification," is connected to the great biblical stories of reversal which point, ultimately, to the "great reversal" of the cross. As such, the narrative and image of Guadalupe belong, most appropriately, in close association with images of the Crucified One Himself. For it is only in light of the image of Christ Crucified, in the image of the cross, where the meaning of Mary—Guadalupe as "the embodiment of God's grace"—is best revealed and appropriated.

We Can Celebrate Mary of Guadalupe Because She Is a Type and Model of What the Church Is to Be in the World

It is not only that the Guadalupan story proclaims the unconditionally gracious, loving, merciful, and compassionate God who justifies the "Juan Diegos" of the world by grace alone through faith. In addition, the very image of Mary of Guadalupe is revelatory of the multiracial, multiethnic, multicultural, *mestiza* "Church" that came to be incarnated as the result of the sixteenth-century cultural confrontation between Spain and Mesoamerica, and still struggles to be born in our own day. Both the person and the image of Mary of Guadalupe, we might say, function as a *typus ecclesiae*, a "type," or "image," or "model" of the Church.

The third reason, then, that we Lutherans can celebrate Mary of Guadalupe is that she is a type and model of what the Church is to be in the world. That is, if the narrative of Mary of Guadalupe can be interpreted correctly as being about justification by grace alone through faith, then the image—which depicts the *typus ecclesiae* herself as pregnant with the Incarnate Word—can surely be seen as, in a mirror reflection, what the Church itself, thanks also to God's unmerited grace, is and is called to be as similarly "pregnant" with the same Incarnate Word for the life and salvation of the world. Indeed, for those who might object that it is precisely *Christ* who appears to be absent from this narrative and image of justification, the words of Virgilio Elizondo in his groundbreaking book *Guadalupe: Mother of the New Creation* need to be heard: "The innermost core of the apparition . . . is what she carries within her womb: the new source and center of the new humanity that is about to be born. And that source and center is Christ as the light and life of the world" (pp. 128–29). And in this sense, then, Mary of Guadalupe is truly "of the gospel" because the narrative and image of Guadalupe are, ultimately, about *Christ*.

Indeed, the interpretation of the image of Mary of Guadalupe as an image and model of the Church itself may be one of the most profound Guadalupan gifts that Mexican and Mexican American spirituality can offer the whole Church catholic in our day. For the Church being called into existence more than ever before is one called to be clearly multicultural and *mestizo* in form, and such a Church of the future appears to be already present proleptically in Mary of Guadalupe's *mestiza* face. To gaze contemplatively upon her image, then, is to gaze at the future Church in the making, and to gaze at what we hope, by God's grace and Spirit, the Church of Jesus Christ, racially, culturally, and even ecumenically, will become.

How appropriate then that we might celebrate Mary of Guadalupe in Advent. For her story and her image are about incarnation, the Incarnation of the gospel, the Good News of God's salvation among us, about our salvation by grace alone through faith, and about who we are and who we are to become as Church in the world. Mary of Guadalupe, pregnant with the Incarnate Word about to be born, belongs to Advent because Mary of Nazareth belongs to Advent and because her Son seeks always to be born anew in us. Former campus chaplain at Gustavus Adolphus College, St. Peter, Minnesota, and Lutheran pastor, the Rev. Richard Q. Elvee, writes of this connection, saying that

> the pregnant Virgin asking Native Americans in a native tongue to become bearers of the Good News of Jesus Christ to the Americas was a powerful experience.

Native peoples, who were being exterminated by foreign disease and decimated by oppression and war, became the bearers of the news that Jesus Christ was waiting to be born in the Americas. . . . These conquered people were to teach their European conquerors the meaning of God's call of faith. These seemingly hopeless people were to become the hope of a hemisphere. With Jesus waiting to be born in the Americas, the Mexican people were to give him a home.

And Professor José David Rodriguez Jr., of the Lutheran School of Theology in Chicago, reminds us that "the story of the Virgin of Guadalupe is part of a broader story of the great saving acts of God in history. The good news for us is that we are invited to be a part of that wonderful and meaningful story."

There may be yet, however, another and very simple reason why we Lutherans would want to celebrate Mary of Guadalupe in this time of preparation for Christ's coming at Christmas. In one of his Christmas Eve sermons Martin Luther once said:

This is the great joy, of which the angel speaks, this is the consolation and the superabundant goodness of God, that man (if he has this faith) may boast of such treasure as that Mary is his real mother, Christ his brother, and God his Father. . . . See to it that you make [Christ's] birth your own, and that you make an exchange with him, so that you rid yourself of your birth and receive instead, his. This happens if you have this faith. By this token you sit assuredly in the Virgin Mary's lap and are her dear child (*Luther's Works*, Fortress Press, vol. 52, pp. 15–16).

Perhaps, then, in the words of both my pizza delivery person and Martin Luther himself, we Lutherans can celebrate Mary of Guadalupe, porque "Ella es nuestra mamá"; because, finally, in faith, "She is also *our* Mom!"

CHAPTER FOURTEEN

~

A Great Sign Appeared in the Sky

Socorro Durán

On Our Lady of Guadalupe's Day I have always been fascinated by the reading taken from the book of Revelation that says, "A great sign appeared in the sky, a woman clothed with the sun, with the moon under her feet, and on her head a crown of twelve stars" (Rev. 12:1). What is this about? For me it speaks of the hope and expectation that Our Lady awakens in us Latinas and Latinos. Like our Native American ancestors we too see a sign of God's presence, God's coming near to us, in sudden and unexpected happenings. A long time ago Our Lady's apparition to Juan Diego was a sudden, unexpected event which then and now brings hope and expectation to us, the descendants of Juan Diego.

Hope is very important, especially when people are discouraged by sickness, poverty, lack of a job, lack of schooling for their children, the insecurity of being undocumented, and on and on. Expectation adds a little possibility and excitement to lives that become sad and burdened by misfortune and oppression. Our situation today is not that different from that of Mexico 475 years ago. There were too many reasons to give up hope then and now. Our situation today and that of our Mexican ancestors is also like the one into which Jesus was born 2,000 years ago. They didn't have many reasons to hope either. That is why Our Lady of Guadalupe for us Mexicans is most definitely an Advent feast. It's more an Advent feast than anything else I can think of that the Church gives us in the Advent liturgies. When we talk about Our Lady of Guadalupe we talk about something we Mexicans know about. Through the story of Guadalupe we have come to experience the hope and expectation that Jesus' coming into the world gives. We have a savior. We are pardoned. We are called to a better life here and beyond.

The hope of the Christmas season we are approaching shows itself on your faces, on the faces of your parents and children when you see the story of Tepeyac re-enacted every year. People just like you play the parts of Juan Diego, the bishop and his attendants, the Virgin, and all the others who appear in the drama. The story is about how the underdog is finally heard. We Latinos are "underdogs," and so we can feel close to Juan Diego, his sick uncle Juan Bernardino, and all his people. The drama of Tepeyac makes you laugh and imagine. You laugh because you see how Juan Diego tries to *dar vueltas*, to avoid the Virgin, but she catches him. You laugh because he becomes so familiar with the Lady that he nicely talks back to her. He becomes like us, a little *rezongón* (grumbler). And you also imagine how it is that God speaks *to you* through this beautiful woman and mother, how God leads *you* forward toward something much better. We want to hear this. We need to hear it. The story of Guadalupe, like the story of Christmas, renews hope in our wilting spirits.

When I think about this feast day I recall those extraordinary scenes of hundreds of people up at 5:00 AM and ready and eager to sing the *mañanitas* to the Virgin. This is what I see right now before me. I see all you families with young children in your arms, so many young people too and, of course, so many of our *viejitos* (elderly). I see workers and *campesinos*, the professional Latinos, the older generations and the recently arrived *mojadito* (immigrant). I also see many Latinos/as from other countries besides Mexico. This day, I imagine, reminds them of the hope they have in another story or image of Mary, the Mother of Jesus, under some other title. But the hope and the expectation are the same. Mary of Guadalupe is the Queen of the Americas, not just of Mexico. That is why year after year I see more and more Anglos here struggling to follow what we say in Spanish but getting the point anyway. Everything we say and do in some way has become for many Anglos "a great sign appearing in the sky." They did not know anything about Our Lady of Guadalupe, but the more they find out and share this celebration with us, the more they want to be with us for these *mañanitas* and Mass. Don't they say we Latinos are *seductive*?

The eagerness of this congregation, your desire to be here, tells me that, if you could, you would be standing now in the plaza of the Basilica of Guadalupe in Mexico City ready to enter and sing "Buenos Días, Paloma Blanca" to the miraculous image from Juan Diego's *tilma* above the main altar of the basilica.

We cannot go there today. But we can show how deep our desire to greet our *Morenita* is with this profusion of flowers that we have brought here this morning. To our ancestors these flowers represented the beauty that is found only in God. We bring beautiful flowers to the beautiful woman who is our Mother. Her beauty, like that of the flowers, takes us to God whom she carries in her womb.

The image of Guadalupe is about new life that is on the way. That is another reason why we are filled with the hope and expectation like that of the young couple who await their first child. They dream how wonderful their lives will be when they bring that new life into the world. That is why Guadalupe is an Advent feast. She reminds us about how God is coming into the world at Christmas.

The story of Guadalupe is too fantastic to just let the priests and preachers talk about it. We all want to talk about it. We must talk about it! We answer our children's questions about what it all means, kind of like the Jewish people at the paschal supper when their children ask, "Why is this feast different from all others?" That was all the Jewish parents needed. Now they can tell the story of what God had done for them when he led them out of slavery in the Exodus. We Mexicans have our own exodus stories. Mary of Guadalupe is our Moses, she calls us forth and keeps us on the pilgrim's path, *el camino del peregrino*. So we share stories of other times in our *pueblitos* when we celebrated the Feast of Guadalupe *como Dios manda*, that is, the *right* way, back in Mexico. Our *abuelitas* (grandmothers) have many stories to tell, and not only about the celebration, but also about how Our Lady has personally been part of their journey, their pain, their struggles, and, of course, their unfading hopes. That is why these words today are meant only as a way to encourage all of you to recall and share what this Virgin and this day have meant to you over a lifetime. Year after year we celebrate and as we do we gather so many wonderful memories of good times, *buenos tiempos*, even in the middle of really bad times. That is why some of us, even the men, may cry—that tells me that this day touches our lives deeply and unforgettably. And that memory fills us with joy and gratitude. It makes us want to live better and fuller lives in the company of family, friends, and loved ones, and in our church, where we gather this morning.

The way this day inspires hope is different for everyone. For me it signals the coming of Christmas. It means that soon we will be gathering on those cold December nights to do the *posadas*. The children will be all excited about the *piñata* and the Guadalupanas will want to know what to serve for refreshments. Already I am smelling the aroma of *tamales dulces* (sweet tamales) and that special *champurrado* (a thick hot chocolate), Doña Chole's specialty. I am thinking about all the community gatherings where we will have time to talk and laugh a little, complain about this and that, listen to some beautiful *villancicos*, but also show in simple and sincere ways that, despite everything, we are a people of hope.

Today's celebration tells me that this is a time of grace when we will share with one another the treasure of our common faith in the God of Jesus Christ. The Son of God was born in time to Mary and today God is born for us again in Mary of Guadalupe. She is the mother of our hope who is Jesus himself. Today we remember that without a mother, there is no son. In the Mass that will follow our *mañanitas* we all will participate in the gift given by the Father who is Jesus himself. And we will find Jesus in *el Padrecito* who leads us in prayer, in the words we read from the Bible, in us—God's people, and in the Holy Communion we will receive. In all of these ways God's life is coming to birth in us. In a special way we will recall the story of Guadalupe after communion time when *el Padrecito* will ask all the women who are pregnant to come forth for a blessing. The great hope we have is that all of us, but especially our children, will be like Christ who was born of Mary. That is why I like the verse from the book of Revelation. Yes, "a great sign appeared in the sky." Today let's open our eyes, look up, and joyfully follow that sign wherever it leads us.

Translated by Allan Figueroa Deck, S.J.

CHAPTER FIFTEEN

A Church of Hope

Pope John Paul II[1]

"When the time had fully come, God sent forth his Son, born of woman" (Gal. 4:4). What is this fullness of time? From the standpoint of human history, the fullness of time is a concrete fact. It is the night when the Son of God came into the world in Bethlehem, as foretold by the prophets and as we have heard in the first reading: "The Lord himself will give you a sign. Behold, a young woman shall conceive and bear a son, and you shall call his name Emmanuel" (Is. 7:14). These words spoken many centuries ago were fulfilled on the night when the Son conceived by the Holy Spirit in the womb of the Virgin Mary entered the world.

Christ's birth was preceded by the message of the angel Gabriel. Afterward Mary went to the home of her cousin Elizabeth to be of service to her. We were reminded of this by the Gospel of Luke, which puts before us Elizabeth's unusual, prophetic greeting and Mary's splendid response: "My soul magnifies the Lord, and my spirit rejoices in God my savior" (1:46–47). These are the events referred to in today's liturgy.

The reading from the Letter to the Galatians, for its part, reveals to us the divine dimension of this fullness of time. The words of the apostle Paul sum up the whole theology of Jesus' birth, at the same time explaining the meaning of this fullness. It is something extraordinary: God has entered human history. God, who in himself is the unfathomable mystery of life; God, who is Father and is himself reflected from all eternity in the Son, consubstantial with him and through whom all things were made (cf. John 1:1, 3); God, who is the unity of the Father and the Son in the flow of eternal love which is the Holy Spirit.

Despite the poverty of our words for expressing the ineffable mystery of the Trinity, the truth is that man, in his temporal condition, has been called to share in this divine life. The Son of God was born of the Virgin Mary to obtain this divine adoption for us. The Father has poured out in our hearts the Spirit of his Son, through whom we can say "Abba, Father!" (cf. Gal. 4:4). Here then is the fullness of time which fulfills all the yearnings of history and of humanity: the revelation of God's mystery, given to human beings through the gift of divine adoption.

The fullness of time to which the apostle refers is related to human history. By becoming man, God in a certain way has entered our time and has transformed our history into the history of salvation. A history that includes all the vicissitudes of the world and of humanity from creation to their conclusion, but advances through important moments and dates. One of them now close at hand is the 2,000th year since the birth of Jesus, the year of the great jubilee, for which the Church has also been preparing by holding extraordinary synods dedicated to each continent such as the one held in the Vatican at the end of 1997.

Today in this basilica of Guadalupe, the Marian heart of America, we thank God for the Special Assembly for America of the Synod of Bishops—a true Upper Room of ecclesial communion and collegial affection among all the pastors from the north, center, and south of the continent, shared with the bishop of Rome as a fraternal experience of encounter with the risen Lord, the way to conversion, communion, and solidarity in America.

Now, one year after the celebration of that synod assembly and in conjunction with the centenary of the plenary council of Latin America held in Rome, I have come here to place at the feet of the *mestiza* Virgin of Tepeyac, star of the New World, the apostolic exhortation *Ecclesia in America*, which incorporates the contributions and pastoral suggestions of that synod, entrusting to the mother and queen of this continent the future of its evangelization.

I wish to express my gratitude to those whose work and prayer enabled that synod assembly to reflect the vitality of the Catholic faith in America. I also thank this primatial Archdiocese of Mexico City and its archbishop, Cardinal Norberto Rivera Carrera, for their cordial welcome and generous cooperation. I affectionately greet the large group of cardinals and bishops who have come from every part of the continent and the great many priests and seminarians present here who fill the pope's heart with joy and hope. My greeting also extends beyond the walls of this basilica to embrace those who are following the celebration from outside, as well as to all the men and women of various cultures, ethnic groups, and nations which form the rich and multifaceted reality of America.

"Blessed is she who believed that there would be a fulfillment of what was spoken to her from the Lord" (Luke 1:45). Elizabeth's words to Mary, who is carrying Christ in her womb, can also be applied to the Church on this continent. Blessed are you, Church in America, for you have welcomed the Good News of the gospel and given birth in faith to numerous peoples! Blessed are you for believing, blessed are you for hoping, blessed are you for loving, because the Lord's promise will be fulfilled!

The heroic missionary efforts and the wonderful evangelization of these five centuries were not in vain. Today we can say that as a result the Church in America is the Church of hope. We need only look at the vigor of her many young people, the exceptional value put on the family, the blossoming of vocations to the priesthood and the consecrated life, and above all, the deep piety of her peoples. Let us not forget that in the next millennium, now close at hand, America will be the continent with the largest number of Catholics.

However, as the synod fathers stressed, if the Church in America has many reasons to rejoice, she also faces serious problems and important challenges. Should we be discouraged by all that? Not at all: "Jesus Christ is Lord!" (Phil. 2:11). He has conquered the world and sent his Holy Spirit to make all things new. Would it be too ambitious to hope that after this synod assembly—the first American synod in history—a more evangelical way of living and sharing would grow on this continent where Christians are the majority? There are many areas where the Christian communities of North, Central, and South America can demonstrate their fraternal ties, practice real solidarity, and collaborate on joint pastoral projects, with each one contributing the spiritual and material wealth at its disposal.

The apostle Paul teaches us that in the fullness of time God sent his Son, born of a woman, to redeem us from sin and to make us his sons and daughters. Accordingly, we are no longer servants but children and heirs of God (cf. Gal. 4:4–7). Therefore, the Church must proclaim the gospel of life and speak out with prophetic force against the culture of death. May the continent of hope also be the continent of life! This is our cry: life with dignity for all! For all who have been conceived in their mother's womb, for street children, for indigenous peoples and Afro-Americans, for immigrants and refugees, for the young deprived of opportunity, for the old, for those who suffer any kind of poverty or marginalization.

Dear brothers and sisters, the time has come to banish once and for all from the continent every attack against life. No more violence, terrorism, and drug trafficking! No more torture or other forms of abuse! There must be an end to the unnecessary recourse to the death penalty! No more exploitation of the weak, racial discrimination, or ghettoes of poverty! Never again! These are intolerable evils which cry out to heaven and call Christians to a different way of living, to a social commitment more in keeping with their faith.

We must rouse the consciences of men and women with the Gospel in order to highlight their sublime vocation as children of God. This will inspire them to build a better America. As a matter of urgency, we must stir up a new springtime of holiness on the continent so that action and contemplation will go hand in hand.

I wish to entrust and offer the future of the continent to Blessed Mary, mother of Christ and of the Church. For this reason, I have the joy now of announcing that I have declared that on December 12 Our Lady of Guadalupe will be celebrated throughout America with the liturgical rank of feast.

O mother! You know the paths followed by the first evangelizers of the New World, from Guanahani Island and Hispaniola to the Amazon forests and the Andean peaks, reaching to Tierra del Fuego in the south and to the Great Lakes and mountains of the north. Accompany the Church, which is working in the nations of America so that she may always preach the Gospel and renew her missionary spirit. Encourage all who devote their lives to the cause of Jesus and the spread of his kingdom.

O gentle lady of Tepeyac, mother of Guadalupe! To you we present this countless multitude of the faithful praying to God in America. You who have penetrated their hearts, visit and comfort the homes, parishes, and dioceses of the whole continent. Grant that Christian families may exemplarily raise their children in the Church's faith and in love of the Gospel, so that they will be the seed of apostolic vocations. Turn your gaze today upon young people and encourage them to walk with Jesus Christ.

O lady and mother of America! Strengthen the faith of our brothers and sisters, so that in all areas of social, professional, cultural, and political life they may act in accord with the truth and the new law which Jesus brought to humanity. Look with mercy on the distress of those suffering from hunger, loneliness, rejection, or ignorance. Make us recognize them as your favorite children and give us the fervent charity to help them in their needs.

Holy Virgin of Guadalupe, queen of peace! Save the nations and peoples of this continent. Teach everyone, political leaders and citizens, to live in true freedom and to act according to the requirements of justice and respect for human rights, so that peace may thus be established once and for all.

To you, O lady of Guadalupe, mother of Jesus and our mother, belong all the love, honor, glory, and endless praise of your American sons and daughters!

Thank you for this splendid gift which I will take with me. I had the joy once again of celebrating in this basilica which is loved so much by all Mexicans, all Americans, children of peace. I thank you for the prayers you offer each day for me and for my Petrine ministry. I know that you will always continue to do so. Thank you.

Notes

1. Pope John Paul II delivered this homily on January 23, 1999, during Mass at the Basilica of Our Lady of Guadalupe in Mexico City. On this occasion he formally presented the apostolic exhortation *Ecclesia in America*, his document based on and responding to the 1997 Special Assembly for America of the Synod of Bishops. This English translation of the original Spanish text first appeared in *Origins* 28 (11 February 1999), and is reprinted here with the permission of *L'Osservatore Romano*.

Appendix: The Text of the *Nican Mopohua*[1]

Here we recount in an orderly way how the Ever-Virgin Holy Mary, Mother of God, our Queen, appeared recently in a marvelous way at Tepeyac, which is called Guadalupe.

Summary

First she allowed herself to be seen by a poor and dignified person whose name is Juan Diego; and then her precious image appeared in the presence of the new bishop D. Fray Juan de Zumárraga. The many marvels that she has brought about are also told.

The Situation of the City and Its Inhabitants

Ten years after the conquest of the City of Mexico, arrows and shields were put down; everywhere the inhabitants of the lake and the mountain had surrendered.

Thus faith started; it gave its first buds; and it flowered in the knowledge of the One through Whom We Live, the true God, Téotl.

Precisely in the year 1531, a few days after the beginning of December, a poor, dignified campesino was in the surroundings [of Tepeyac]. His name was Juan Diego. It was said that his home was in Cuauhtitlán.

And insofar as the things of God, all that region belonged to Tlatelolco.

First Encounter with the Virgin

It was Saturday, when it was still night. He was going in search of the things of God and of God's messages. And when he arrived at the side of the small hill, which was named Tepeyac, it was already beginning to dawn.

He heard singing on the summit of the hill: as if different precious birds were singing and their songs would alternate, as if the hill was answering them. Their song was most pleasing and very enjoyable, better than that of the coyoltotol or of the tzinizcan or of the other precious birds that sing.

Juan Diego stopped and said to himself: "By chance do I deserve this? Am I worthy of what I am hearing? Maybe I am dreaming? Maybe I only see this in my dreams? Where am I? Maybe I am in the land of my ancestors, of the elders, of our grandparents? In the Land of Flower, in the Earth of our flesh? Maybe over there inside of heaven?"

His gaze was fixed on the summit of the hill, toward the direction from which the sun arises: the beautiful celestial song was coming from there to here. And when the song finally ceased, when everything was calm, he heard that he was being called from the summit of the hill. He heard: "Dignified Juan, dignified Juan Diego."

Then he dared to go where he was being called. His heart was in no way disturbed, and in no way did he experience any fear; on the contrary, he felt very good, very happy.

He went to the top of the hill, and he saw a lady who was standing and who was calling him to come closer to her side. When he arrived in her presence, he marveled at her perfect beauty. Her clothing appeared like the sun, and it gave forth rays.

And the rock and the cliffs where she was standing, upon receiving the rays like arrows of light, appeared like precious emeralds, appeared like jewels; the earth glowed with the splendors of the rainbow. The mesquites, the cacti, and the weeds that were all around appeared like feathers of the quetzal, and the stems looked like turquoise; the branches, the foliage, and even the thorns sparkled like gold.

He bowed before her, heard her thought and word, which were exceedingly re-creative, very ennobling, alluring, producing love. She said "Listen, my most abandoned son, dignified Juan: Where are you going?"

And he answered: "My Owner and My Queen: I have to go to your house of Mexico-Tlatelolco, to follow the divine things that our priests, who are the images of our Lord, give to us." Then she conversed with him and unveiled her precious will. She said: "Know and be certain in your heart, my most abandoned son, that I am the Ever-Virgin Holy Mary, Mother of the God of Great Truth, Téotl, of the One through Whom We Live, the Creator of Persons, the Owner of What Is Near and Together, of the Lord of Heaven and Earth.

"I very much want and ardently desire that my hermitage be erected in this place. In it I will show and give to all people all my love, my compassion, my help, and my protection, because I am your merciful mother and the mother of all the nations that live on this earth who would love me, who would speak with me, who would search for me, and who would place their confidence in me. There I will hear their laments and remedy and cure all their miseries, misfortunes, and sorrows.

"And for this merciful wish of mine to be realized, go there to the palace of the bishop of Mexico, and you will tell him in what way I have sent you as messenger, so that you may make known to him how I very much desire that he build me a home right here, that he may erect my temple on the plain. You will tell him carefully everything you have seen and admired and heard.

"Be absolutely certain that I will be grateful and will repay you; and because of this I will make you joyful; I will give you happiness; and you will earn much that will repay you for your trouble and your work in carrying out what I have entrusted to you. Look, my son the most abandoned one, you have heard my statement and my word; now do everything that relates to you."

Then he bowed before her and said to her: "My Owner and my Queen, I am already on the way to make your statement and your word a reality. And now I depart from you, I your poor servant." Then he went down to the road that leads directly to Mexico [City].

First Interview with the Bishop

Having entered the city, he went directly to the palace of the bishop, who had recently arrived as the lord of the priests; his name was Don Fray Juan de Zumárraga, a priest of Saint Francis.

As soon as he [Juan Diego] arrived, he tried to see him [the lord bishop]. He begged his servants, his attendants, to go speak to him. After a long time, they came to call him, telling him that the lord bishop had ordered him to come in. As soon as he entered, he prostrated himself and then knelt. Immediately he presented, he revealed, the thought and the word of the Lady from Heaven and her will. And he also told him everything he had admired, seen, and heard. When he [the bishop] heard all his words, his message, it was as if he didn't give it much credibility. He answered him and told him: "My son, you will have to come another time. I still have to see, to examine carefully from the very beginning, the reason you have come, and your will and your wish."

He felt very saddened because in no way whatsoever had her message been accomplished.

Second Encounter with the Virgin

The same day, he returned [to Tepeyac]. He came to the summit of the hill and found the Lady from Heaven: she was waiting in the very same spot where he had seen her the first time.

When he saw her, he prostrated himself before her, he fell upon the earth and said: "My Owner, my Matron, my Lady, the most abandoned of my Daughters, my Child, I went where you sent me to deliver your thought and your word. With great difficulty I entered the place of the lord of the priests; I saw him; before him I expressed your thought and word, just as you had ordered me. He received me well and listened carefully. But by the way he answered me, as if his heart had not accepted it, [I know] he did not believe it. He told me: 'You will have to come another time; I will calmly listen to you at another time. I still have to see, to examine carefully from the very beginning, the reason you have come, and your will and your wish.' I saw perfectly, in the way he answered me, that he thinks that possibly I am just making it up that you want a temple to be built on this site, and possibly it is not your command.

"Hence, I very much beg you, my Owner, my Queen, my Child, that you charge one of the more valuable nobles, a well-known person, one who is respected and esteemed, to come by and take your message and your word so that he may be believed. Because in reality I am one of those campesinos, a piece of rope, a small ladder, the excrement of people; I am a leaf; they order me around, lead me by force; and you, my most abandoned Daughter, my Child, my Lady, and my Queen, send me to a place where I do not belong. Forgive me, I will cause pain to your countenance and to your heart; I will displease you and fall under your wrath, my Lady and my Owner."

The ever-venerated Virgin answered: "Listen, my most abandoned son, know well in your heart that there are not a few of my servants and messengers to whom I could give the mandate of taking my thought and my word so that my will may be accomplished. But it is absolutely necessary that you personally go and speak about this, and that precisely through your mediation and help, my wish and my desire be realized. I beg you very much, my most abandoned son, and with all my energy I command that precisely tomorrow you go again to see the bishop. In my name you will make him know, make him listen well to my wish and desire, so that he may make my wish a reality and build my temple. And tell him once again that I personally, the Ever-Virgin Mary, the Mother of the God Téotl, am the one who is sending you there."

Juan Diego answered her: "My Owner, my Lady, my Child, I will not cause pain to your countenance and your heart. With a very good disposition of my heart, I will go; there I will go to tell him truthfully your thought and your word. In no way whatsoever will I fail to do it; it will not be painful for me to go. I will go to do your will. But it could well be that I will not be listened to; and if I am listened to, possibly I will not be believed. Tomorrow in the afternoon, when the sun sets, I will return your thought and word to you, what the lord of the priests [has] answer[ed] me.

"Now I take leave of you, my most abandoned Daughter, my Child, my Matron, my Lady, now you rest a bit." Then he went to his home to rest.

Second Interview with the Bishop

The next day, Sunday, when it was still night, when it was still dark, he left his home and went directly to Tlatelolco to learn about the things divine, and to answer roll call so that afterward he could see the lord of priests.

Around ten in the morning, when they had gathered together and heard mass and answered roll call and the poor had been dispersed, Juan Diego went immediately to the house of the lord bishop.

And when he arrived there, he made every effort to see him, and with great difficulty he succeeded in seeing him. He knelt at his feet; he cried and became very sad as he was communicating and unveiling before him the thought and the word of the Lady from Heaven, hoping to be accepted as her messenger and believing that it was the will of the Ever Virgin to have him build a dwelling in the place where she wanted it.

But the lord bishop asked him many questions; he interrogated him as to where he saw her and all about her so as to satisfy his heart. And he told the lord bishop everything.

But even though he told him everything, all about her figure, all that he had seen and admired, and how she had shown herself to be the lovable Ever

Virgin and admirable mother of our Lord and Savior Jesus Christ, yet, he still did not believe him.

He [the bishop] told him that he could not proceed on her wishes just on the basis of his word and message. A sign from her would be necessary for the bishop to believe that he [Juan Diego] was indeed sent by the Lady from Heaven. When Juan Diego heard this he told the bishop: "My patron and my lord, what is the sign that you want? [When I know, I can] go and ask the Lady from Heaven, she who sent me here." The bishop was impressed that he was so firm in the truth, that he did not doubt anything or hesitate in any way. He dismissed him.

And when he had left, he [the lord bishop] sent some people from his household in whom he trusted, to follow him and observe where he went, what he saw, and with whom he was speaking. And so it was done. And Juan Diego went directly down the road. His followers took the same route. Close to the bridge of Tepeyac, in the hillside, they lost sight of him; they kept looking for him everywhere, but they could not find him anyplace.

Thus they returned infuriated and were angered at him because he frustrated their intentions. In this state of mind, they went to inform the lord bishop, creating in him a bad attitude so that he would not believe him; they told him that he was only deceiving him; that he was only imagining what he was coming to say; that he was only dreaming; or that he had invented what he was coming to tell him. They agreed among themselves that if he were to come again, they would grab him and punish him harshly, so that he would not lie again or deceive the people.

Juan Diego Takes Care of His Uncle

On the next day, Monday, when Juan Diego was supposed to take something to be the sign by which he was to be believed, he did not return, because when he arrived home, one of his uncles, named Juan Bernardino, had caught the smallpox and was in his last moments.

First he went to call a doctor, who helped him, but he could do no more because he [Juan Bernardino] was already gravely ill. Through the night, his uncle begged him that while it was still dark, he should go to Tlatelolco to call a priest to come and hear his confession and prepare him well because he felt deeply in his heart that this was the time and place of his death, that he would not be healed.

Third Encounter with the Virgin

And on Tuesday, when it was still night, Juan Diego left his home to go to Tlatelolco to call a priest.

And when he arrived at the side of Mount Tepeyac at the point where the road leads out, on the side on which the sun sets, the side he was accustomed to take, he said: "If I take this road, it is quite possible that the Lady will come to see me as before and will hold me back so that I may take the sign to the lord of the priests as she had instructed me. But first I must attend to our affliction and quickly call the priest. My uncle is agonizing and is waiting for him."

He then went around the hill; he climbed through the middle; and he went to the other side, to the side of the sunrise, so as to arrive quickly into Mexico, and to avoid the Lady from Heaven delaying him. He thought that having taken this other route, he would not be seen by the one who cares for everyone.

He saw her coming down from the top of the hill; and from there, where he had seen her before, she had been watching him. She came to him at the side of the hill, blocked his passage, and, standing in front of him, said: "My most abandoned son, where are you going? In what direction are you going?"

Did he become embarrassed a bit? Was he ashamed? Did he feel like running away? Was he fearful? He bowed before her, greeted her, and said: "My Child, my most abandoned Daughter, my Lady, I hope you are happy. How did the dawn come upon you? Does your body feel all right, my Owner and my Child? I am going to give great pain to your countenance and heart. You must know, my Child, that my uncle, a poor servant of yours, is in his final agony; a great illness has fallen upon him, and because of it he will die.

"I am in a hurry to get to your house in Mexico; I am going to call one of the beloved of our Lord, one of our priests, so that he may go and hear his confession and prepare him. Because for this have we been born, to await the moment of our death. But if right now I am going to do this, I will quickly return here; I will come back to take your thought and your word. My Matron, and my Child, forgive me, have a little patience with me; I do not want to deceive you, my most abandoned Daughter, my Child. Tomorrow I will come quickly."

After hearing Juan Diego's discourse, the most pious Virgin answered: "Listen and hear well in your heart, my most abandoned son: that which scares you and troubles you is nothing; do not let your countenance and heart be troubled; do not fear that sickness or any other sickness or anxiety. Am I not here, your mother? Are you not under my shadow and my protection? Am I not your source of life? Are you not in the hollow of my mantle where I cross my arms? Who else do you need? Let nothing trouble you or cause you sorrow. Do not worry because of your uncle's sickness. He will not die of his present sickness. Be assured in your heart that he is already healed." (And as he learned later on, at that precise moment, his uncle was healed.)

When Juan Diego heard the thought and word of the Lady from Heaven, he was very much consoled; his heart became peaceful. He begged her to send him immediately to see the lord of the priests to take him his sign, the thing that would bring about the fulfillment of her desire, so that he would be believed.

Then the Lady from Heaven sent him to climb to the top of the hill where he had seen her before. She said to him: "Go up, my most abandoned son, to the top of the hill, and there, where you saw me and I gave you my instructions, there you will see many diverse flowers: cut them, gather them, put them together. Then come down here and bring them before me."

Juan Diego climbed the hill, and when he arrived at the top, he was deeply surprised. All over the place there were all kinds of exquisite flowers from Castile, open and flowering. It was not a place for flowers, and likewise it was the time when the ice hardens upon the earth. They were very fragrant, as if they were filled with fine pearls, filled with the morning dew. He started to cut them; he gathered then; he placed them in the hollow of his mantle. And the top of the hill was certainly not a place where flowers grew; there were only rocks, thistles, thorns, cacti, mesquites; and if small herbs grew there, during the month of December, they were all eaten up and wilted by the ice.

Immediately he went down; he went to take to the Queen of Heaven the various flowers that he had cut. When she saw them, she took them in her small hands; and then he placed them in the hollow of his mantle.

And she told him: "My most abandoned son, these different flowers are the proof, the sign, that you will take to the bishop. In my name tell him that he is to see in them what I want, and with this he should carry out my wish and my will.

"And you, you are my ambassador; in you I place all my trust. With all my strength I command you that only in the presence of the bishop are you to open your mantle, and let him know and reveal to him what you are carrying. You will recount everything well; you will tell him how I sent you to climb to the top of the hill to go cut the flowers, and all that you saw and admired. With this you will change the heart of the lord of the priests so that he will do his part to build and erect my temple that I have asked him for."

As soon as the Lady from Heaven had given him her command, he immediately took to the road that leads to Mexico. He was in a hurry and very happy; his heart felt very sure and secure; he was carrying with great care what he knew would [bring about] a good end. He was very careful with that which he carried in the hollow of his mantle, lest anything would fall out. He was enjoying the scent of the beautiful flowers.

Third Interview with the Bishop and the Apparition of the Virgin

Upon arriving at the palace of the bishop, he ran into the doorkeepers and the other servants of the king of the priests. He begged them to go tell him [the bishop] that he wanted to see him; but none of them wanted to; they did not want to pay attention to him, both because it was still night and they knew him: he was the one who only bothered them and gave them long faces; and also because their fellow workers had told them how they had lost him from their sight when they had been following him. He waited a very long time.

When they saw that he had been standing with his head lowered (very sad) for a long time, that he was waiting in vain for them to call him, and that it seemed that he carried something in the hollow of his mantle, they approached him to see what he had and satisfy their hearts.

And when Juan Diego saw that it was impossible to hide from them what he was carrying, that he would be punished for this, that they would throw him out or mistreat him, he showed them just a little of the flowers.

When they saw that they were all different flowers from Castile and that it was not the season for flowers, they were very astonished, especially by the fact that they were in full bloom, so fresh, so fragrant, and very beautiful. Three times they tried to grab some of them and take them from him, but they could not do it because when they were about to grab them, they did not see any more real flowers, but only painted or embroidered ones, or flowers sewn in his mantle.

Immediately they went to tell the lord bishop what they had seen, and that the poor little Indian who had already come many times wanted to see him, and that he had been waiting for a very long time. Upon hearing this, the lord bishop realized this meant the despicable man had the proof to convince him and bring about what he was coming to ask for.

Immediately he ordered that he be brought in to see him. As soon as he [Juan Diego] entered, he knelt before him [the bishop] as he had done before, and once again he told him everything he had seen and admired and also her message.

He said to him: "My owner and my lord, I have accomplished what you asked for; I went to tell my Matron, my Owner, the Lady from Heaven, Holy Mary, the precious Mother of God Téotl, how you had asked me for a sign in order to believe me, so that you might build her temple where she is asking you to erect it. And besides, I told her that I had given you my word that I would bring you a sign and a proof of her will that you want to receive from my hands. When she received your thought and your word, she accepted willingly what you asked for, a sign and a proof so that her desire and will may come about.

"And today when it was still night, she sent me to come and see you once again. But I asked her for the sign and the proof of her will that you asked me for and she had agreed to give to me. Immediately she complied.

"She sent me to the top of the hill, where I had seen her before, so that there I might cut the flowers from Castile. After I had cut them, I took them to the bottom of the hill. And she, with her precious little hands, took them; she arranged them in the hollow of my mantle, so that I might bring them to you, and deliver them to you personally. Even though I knew well that the top of the hill was not a place where flowers grow, that only stones, thistles, thorns, cacti, and mesquites abound there, I still was neither surprised nor doubted. As I was arriving at the top of the hill, my eyes became fixed: It was the Flowering Earth! It was covered with all kinds of flowers from Castile, full of dew and shining brilliantly. Immediately I went to cut them. And she told me why I had to deliver them to you; so that you might see the sign you requested and so that you will believe in her will; and also so that the truth of my word and my message might be manifested. Here they are. Please receive them."

He unfolded his white mantle, the mantle in whose hollow he had gathered the flowers he had cut, and at that instant the different flowers from Castile fell to the ground. In that very moment she painted herself: the precious image of the Ever-Virgin Holy Mary, Mother of the God Téotl, appeared suddenly, just as she is today and is kept in her precious home, in her hermitage of Tepeyac, which is called Guadalupe.

Conversion of the Bishop

When the lord bishop saw her, he and all who accompanied him fell to their knees and were greatly astonished. They stood up to see her; they became saddened; their hearts and their minds became very heavy.

The lord bishop, with tears and sadness, prayed to her and begged her to forgive him for not having believed her will, her heart, and her word.

When he stood up, he untied the mantle from Juan Diego's neck, the mantle in which had appeared and was painted the Lady from Heaven. Then he took her and went to place her in his oratory.

The Construction of the Hermitage

Juan Diego spent one more day in the home of the bishop, who had invited him [to stay]. And on the next day he said, "Let us go to see where it is the will of the Lady from Heaven that the hermitage be built."

Immediately people were invited to construct and build it. And when Juan Diego showed where the Lady from Heaven had indicated that the hermitage should be built, he asked permission to leave. He wanted to go home to see his uncle Juan Bernardino, the one who had been in his final agony, whom he had left to go to Tlatelolco to call a priest to come, hear his confession, and prepare him well, the one who, the Lady from Heaven had said, had been healed. But they did not let him go alone; they accompanied him to his home.

The Fourth Apparition and First Miracle

When they arrived, they saw his uncle who was well and with no pains. He [Juan Bernardino] was very much surprised that his nephew was so well accompanied and honored, and he asked him why they were honoring him so much.

He told him how when he had left him to go call a priest to come to hear his confession and prepare him well, the Queen of Heaven appeared to him over there, at Tepeyac, and sent him to Mexico to see the lord bishop so that he would build her a home at Tepeyac. And she told him not to be troubled because his uncle was healed, and he was very consoled.

And the uncle said that this was true, that it was precisely then that she had healed him, and he had seen her exactly as she had shown herself to his nephew, and that she had told him that he [Juan Bernardino] had to go to

Mexico to see the bishop. And [she told him] also that when he went to see the bishop, he would reveal all that he had seen and would tell him in what a marvelous way she had healed him and that he [the bishop] would call and name that precious image the Ever-Virgin Holy Mary of Guadalupe.

They took Juan Bernardino to the bishop so that he might speak and witness before him. And, together with his nephew Juan Diego, he was hosted by the bishop in his home for several days, until the hermitage of the Queen and Lady from Heaven was built at Tepeyac, where Juan Diego had seen her.

The Entire City before the Virgin

And the lord bishop transferred to the major church the precious image of the Queen and Lady from Heaven; he took her from the oratory of his palace so that all might see and venerate her precious image.

The entire city was deeply moved; they came to see and admire her precious image as something divine; they came to pray to her. They admired very much how she had appeared as a divine marvel, because absolutely no one on earth had painted her precious image.

Notes

1. This English translation of the *Nican Mopohua*, the Nahuatl Guadalupe apparition narrative, is taken from Virgilio Elizondo's *Guadalupe: Mother of the New Creation* (Orbis, 1997), which also contains an extensive commentary on the various details and theological significance of this sacred text. Section headings are not part of the original text but are included here to assist the reader.

Further Reading

Brodeur, Raymond. *Antonio Valeriano, Nican Mopohua, traduction et presentation*. Trévoux: La compagnie de Trévoux, 2003.

Davis, Kenneth G., and Jorge L. Presmanes, eds. *Preaching and Culture in Latino Congregations*. Chicago: Liturgy Training Publications, 2000.

Deck, Allan Figueroa. *The Second Wave: Hispanic Ministry and the Evangelization of Cultures*. New York: Paulist, 1989.

De Luna, Anita. *Faith Formation and Popular Religion: Lessons from the Tejano Experience*. Lanham, MD: Rowman and Littlefield, 2002.

Elizondo, Virgilio. *Guadalupe: Mother of the New Creation*. Maryknoll, NY: Orbis, 1997.

———. *La Morenita: Evangelizer of the Americas*. San Antonio: Mexican American Cultural Center Press, 1980.

Elizondo, Virgilio, and Friends. *A Retreat with Our Lady of Guadalupe and Juan Diego: Heeding the Call*. Cincinnati: St. Anthony Messenger Press, 1998.

García Rivera, Alejandro. *The Community of the Beautiful: A Theological Aesthetics*. Collegeville, MN: Liturgical Press, 1999.

Groody, Daniel G. *Border of Death, Valley of Life: An Immigrant Journey of Heart and Spirit*. Lanham, MD: Rowman and Littlefield, 2002.

Icaza, Rosa María, ed. *Faith Expressions of Hispanics in the Southwest*. Third revised edition. San Antonio: Mexican American Cultural Center Press, 2003.

Isasi-Díaz, Ada María, Timoteo Matovina, and Nina M. Torres-Vidal. *Camino a Emaús: Compartiendo el ministerio de Jesús*. Minneapolis, MN: Augsburg Fortress and Collegeville, MN: Liturgical Press, 2002.

Johnson, Maxwell. *The Virgin of Guadalupe: Theological Reflections of an Anglo-Lutheran Liturgist*. Lanham, MD: Rowman and Littlefield, 2002.

Matovina, Timothy. *Guadalupe and Her Faithful: Latino Catholics in San Antonio, from Colonial Origins to the Present*. Baltimore: Johns Hopkins University Press, 2005.

Rodriguez, Jeanette. *Our Lady of Guadalupe: Faith and Empowerment among Mexican American Women*. Austin: University of Texas Press, 1994.

———. *Stories We Live/Cuentos que vivimos: Hispanic Women's Spirituality*. New York: Paulist, 1996.

Schulte, Francisco Raymond. *Mexican Spirituality: Its Sources and Mission in the Earliest Guadalupan Sermons*. Lanham, MD: Rowman and Littlefield, 2002.

~

Illustration Credits

Ruben Alfaro, pp. x, 24, 44, 108

Cheryl Kelly, p. xviii

University of Texas Institute of Texan Cultures, San Antonio, Texas, pp. 10, 64, 72, 96

Sister Dominic Garcia, M.C.D.P., p. 18

Brother Claude Lane, O.S.B., pp. 30, 38, 58, 86, 102

Daniel Groody, C.S.C., p. 50

Snite Museum of Art, University of Notre Dame, p. 80

Index

About the Editors and Contributors

Raymond Brodeur teaches religious education and catechetical theology at the Université Laval in Québec, Canada, and is a leader in a research group on mystical spirituality for the Centre d'Études Marie de l'Incarnation. He holds a doctorate in theology from the Institut Catholique and a doctorate in religious sciences from the Sorbonne, both in Paris. Dr. Brodeur became fascinated with Our Lady of Guadalupe when he spent a sabbatical year at the Mexican American Cultural Center in San Antonio, Texas.

Allan Figueroa Deck, S.J., holds doctoral degrees in Latin American studies from Saint Louis University and in missiology from the Gregorian University. He has held faculty positions at the Jesuit School of Theology at Berkeley and at Loyola Marymount University in Los Angeles and currently serves as president of the Loyola Institute for Spirituality in Orange, California. A leading speaker and writer on Hispanic theology and ministry for three decades, he was the cofounder and first president of national organizations such as the Academy of Catholic Hispanic Theologians of the United States (ACHTUS) and the National Catholic Council for Hispanic Ministry (NCCHM).

Anita de Luna, M.C.D.P., teaches theology and is director of the Women's Center at Our Lady of the Lake University in San Antonio, Texas. She is nationally recognized for her work as a theologian and a catechist and was the first Latina sister elected to serve as president of the Leadership Conference of Women Religious (LCWR). Her various publications include the recent book *Faith Formation and Popular Religion: Lessons from the Tejano Experience.*

Mary Doak is on the faculty of theology at the University of Notre Dame, where she teaches various courses on systematic theology that encompass the writings of Latina and Latino theologians. Her most recent major publication is *Reclaiming Narrative for Public Theology*.

Socorro Durán has been the director of Hispanic ministry at St. Leander's parish in northern California for more than thirty years. She pioneered ministry to victims of HIV/AIDS in the Oakland diocese. Born in Mexico and raised across the street from the Guadalupe Basilica, she has great fondness for everything related to *La Morenita*.

Virgilio Elizondo is internationally renowned for his pastoral leadership and theological reflection on Our Lady of Guadalupe, *mestizaje*, and the Galilean Jesus. He was the founder and first president of the Mexican American Cultural Center in San Antonio and has authored numerous articles and books, among the most recent *Guadalupe: Mother of the New Creation*. A priest of the archdiocese of San Antonio, Elizondo currently directs the archdiocesan television ministry and teaches theology at the University of Notre Dame.

David García is the rector of San Antonio's acclaimed San Fernando Cathedral, where he has been the driving force in a major cathedral renovation and outreach expansion project. A San Antonio diocesan priest for more than thirty years, García is also noted for his writings and work in vocations, community organizing, and the faith expressions of Mexican Americans.

Cecilia González-Andrieu is a writer, media artist, and theologian whose artistic and scholarly work centers on the interlacing of the arts and theology. Currently she is completing a doctorate at the Graduate Theological Union, Berkeley, and is an award-winning essayist for *The Tidings*, the newspaper of the Archdiocese of Los Angeles. Her documentary and dramatic radio and television projects feature U.S. Latino culture and religion with an emphasis on social justice and the liberating power of art.

Rosa María Icaza, C.C.V.I., has dedicated herself to service on the faculty and program administration of the Mexican American Cultural Center for over twenty-five years. A past winner of the Archbishop Patricio Flores Award for outstanding contributions to Hispanic ministry and a former president of the Instituto Nacional Hispano de Liturgia, she is renowned for her translations of liturgical texts and other official documents. She has also long been a member of the Sub-committee for Liturgy in Spanish of the Bishops' Committee for Liturgy and has authored and delivered numerous presentations on Guadalupe and other Mexican American religious traditions, especially her updated version of the collective volume *Faith Expressions of Hispanics in the Southwest*.

Pope John Paul II is fondly remembered by many devotees of Our Lady of Guadalupe for his pastoral vision, canonization of St. Juan Diego, and moving reflections and tributes to their patroness and mother in Mexico, the Vatican, and throughout the Americas.

Maxwell E. Johnson is professor of theology at the University of Notre Dame, where he is the coordinator of the liturgical studies area. An ordained minister in the Evangelical Lutheran Church in America, he is a frequent contributor to scholarly journals and the author of twelve books, including his recent *The Virgin of Guadalupe: Theological Reflections of an Anglo-Lutheran Liturgist*.

Timothy Matovina teaches theology and is the William and Anna Jean Cushwa Director of the Cushwa Center for the Study of American Catholicism at the University of Notre Dame. His presentations and writings focus on theology and culture, particularly Latino Catholicism in the United States, and include the recent book *Guadalupe and Her Faithful: Latino Catholics in San Antonio, from Colonial Origins to the Present*.

Verónica Méndez, R.C.D., was born in Puerto Rico and raised in El Barrio, Spanish Harlem, New York City. She has served Hispanic communities from Florida to Chicago to New York. As director of Spanish Projects for RENEW International, she ministers in leadership training and adult faith formation with the Spanish-speaking population of the United States.

Jorge L. Presmanes, O.P., is an assistant professor of theology at Barry University in Miami. He teaches U.S. Hispanic Popular Religious Expressions at the Southeast Pastoral Institute and is the coeditor of the book, *Preaching and Culture in Latino Congregations*. He is also the former pastor of St. Dominic Church, a large Latino parish in Miami.

Anastacio Rivera, S.J., born and raised in Arizona, and now a Jesuit priest in the California Province of the Society of Jesus, is assistant director of the

Loyola Institute for Spirituality in Orange, California. A popular director for retreats, parish missions, and conferences in English and Spanish, he is also the coordinator for the Equipo Latino Ignaciano, a Spanish-language training program for persons who wish to engage in the spirituality ministries of the Institute. He has long been fascinated with the *Nican Mopohua* apparition accounts about Guadalupe and is a frequent speaker on the Guadalupan encounter and other topics related to Latino faith and spirituality.

Jeanette Rodriguez is professor of theology and chair of the Theology and Religious Studies Department at Seattle University, a member of the National Board of Pax Christi, and a past president of the Academy of Catholic Hispanic Theologians of the United States (ACHTUS). She is the author of *Our Lady of Guadalupe: Faith and Empowerment among Mexican American Women*; *Stories We Live*; and numerous articles on U.S. Hispanic theology, spirituality, and cultural memory.